T0197257

Incurable:

The Haunted Writings of Lionel Johnson, the Decadent Era's Dark Angel

Edited by Nina Antonia

First published by Strange Attractor Press in 2018.

Print on Demand edition 2024.

Introduction © Nina Antonia 2018

ISBN 978-1-907222-62-7

Distributed by The MIT Press, Cambridge, Massachusetts.
And London, England.

STRANGE ATTRACTOR PRESS

BM SAP, LONDON, WC1N 3XX, UK

WWW.STRANGEATTRACTOR.CO.UK

INCURABLE

The Haunted Writings of Lionel Johnson,
the Decadent Era's Dark Angel

Edited by Nina Antonia

Frontispiece to *Poems* (1895), designed by Herbert Horne.

CONTENTS

RITUALISTIC ADORABILITIES
Nina Antonia

He has renounced the world and built up a twilight world instead, where all the colours are like colours in the rainbow that is cast by the Moon, and all the people, as the people upon faded and dropping tapestries... He has made a world full of altar lights and golden vestures, and murmured Latin and incense clouds, and Autumn winds and dead leaves, where one wanders remembering martyrdoms that the world has forgotten.
W.B. Yeats

He was a spiritual rebel, a spiritual waif who couldn't endure the truth, but demanded a lovelier fiction to revel in, invented it or accepted it, and called it revelation. In part like Shelley, in part like Rimbaud, he despised the world and adored the unreal.
George Santayana

Lionel Johnson is the shadow man of the 1890s, "Pale as wasted golden hair" ('Trentals' 1889) who haunted his own brief life and the memories of those dearest to him. Despite being a major influence on W.B. Yeats, a noted poet and a close associate of Lord Alfred Douglas and Oscar Wilde, his legacy is curiously ephemeral. An elusive, ascetic figure who became increasingly reclusive, Lionel found solace in alcohol, Catholicism and mystical idylls. A solitary visionary, his muse was the fathomless reaches:

> A voice on the winds
> A voice by the waters
> Wanders and cries:
> *Oh what are the winds?*
> *And what are the waters?*
> *Mine are your eyes!*
> 'To Morfydd' 1891

It has been easy for Lionel Johnson to slip away, a refined little wraith who would have been horrified by his own alcoholic decline, no matter how polite his manners remained as he tumbled out of life and cultural circulation. Any interest since Lionel's death at the age of 35, in 1902, has been marginal and academic, an irony given that his was the poetry of things forgotten. Acting as Johnson's sole torch bearer, the late Dr Iain Fletcher wrote insightful introductions to several limited edition anthologies but there has been precious little else.

One would be mistaken in thinking that Lionel's work is inaccessible. He could be as mischievous as Puck, as his best essays attest, whilst his poetry has a spectral desolation that still rings true across the years. Yet in spite of his import, both creatively and as a social catalyst, Lionel has thus far evaded reclamation, unlike his drinking companion, Ernest Dowson.

Enshrined by W.B. Yeats as the figureheads of The Tragic Generation of poets, Dowson's romanticised myth has flourished whilst Lionel remains as ethereal as a half drawn figure in shade. As the author Katharine Tynan noted:

His ghostliness was the ghostliness of a little monk: you might have seen his slight figure flit through a haunted cloister by moonlight. He was shadowy. Somehow he made ordinary flesh and blood seem rough, positive and jarring. (*Memories* 1924)

An unexpected early evening snow storm in Broadstairs, Kent, heralded the birth of Lionel Johnson on March 15th, 1867. Lionel's father, Captain William Victor Johnson, had retired from the 90th Light Infantry and occupied himself constructing additional wings to the family home, King's Mead, which nestled in splendid seclusion in Windsor Forest. The Captain had started building the house in 1860, when he'd married a barrister's daughter, Catherine Delicia Walters. Together they would sire four children, Lionel being the youngest.

A sense of duty pervaded King's Mead, the rather jolly name of the house at odds with a regime of rigid piety: "As you see, faith is in my family" Lionel was to report, "my father with his 'omnipotent', my mother with her churchism." (*Winchester Letters*, 1919) Unfortunately for Lionel, his mother was to adopt a "gruesomely apocalyptic" outlook that prevented him from inviting friends back to the house. (Letter to Campbell Dodgson) Details of Johnson's earliest years are scant though telling: "As a child, I found one of my chief pleasures in secretly pulling to pieces the Bible." (*Winchester Letters*)

However, the first residence where Lionel found emotional succour was Winchester College, which he attended between the ages of 13 and 18, after winning a scholarship. Established in the mid-thirteenth century by William Wykeham and set in acres of ravishing countryside, Winchester is one of England's most ancient and prestigious schools, a medieval old-world dream into which Lionel gladly wandered. Social ease was ensured as young master Johnson hailed from a lineage of respected gentry that included a Baronet and a general. Winchester College was to remain emblazoned on Lionel Johnson's heart and poetry: "To the dearest! Ah to thee! Hast thou not in all to me/Mother, more than mother, been?" ('Winchester' 1888)

Of delicate health and slight stature, Lionel was never to grow beyond five foot three inches and was unable to follow the family tradition of an army career; his older brothers, Victor George Ralph Johnson (1861-1915) and Hugh Walters Beaumont Johnson (1865-1916), both attained the rank of Captain, like their father. Consequently, Lionel was to quip that the only military role he would have been fit for was that of drummer boy, an unfortunate post as they were often the first to die in battle. Lionel was the changeling in the nest, noting of his father "He cannot understand what I feel and I cannot explain or dissect my soul." (*Winchester Letters*)

Although a later sympathy evolved for his middle brother, Hugh, when he fell into debt and became suicidal, Lionel perceived the instilling of comfort as a spiritual duty. Little is known of his sister, Isabella, though she remained unmarried and was to outlive all of her siblings. Lionel did form a significant alliance with his cousin, Olivia Tucker; not only were they dear friends but both were passionate about Shelley, one of Lionel's early poetic deities. "I *do* know Shelley" Johnson was to write whilst still a schoolboy… "I know only too well 'the wide, grey, lampless deep, unpeopled world'".

Despite his reserve, Lionel regularly corresponded with a trinity of friends: Jack Badley, Francis, Earl Russell and Charles Sayle. In 1919, Lionel's college dispatches were anonymously edited by Francis Russell for publication as *Some Winchester Letters* via George Allen. The book's emotional preface shows that Lionel was able to inspire lasting affection in those he reached out to from his lofty, cloud shrouded turret, Russell commenting: "I recognise that I was often chilled by this aloofness, although I believe as far as his nature permitted it, he was fond of me."

In spite of Russell's clumsy editing, *Some Winchester Letters* provides insight into the blossoming of a singularly picturesque character. What Lionel couldn't make up for in physical prowess he overcame with a prodigious capacity for knowledge and a yearning for the sublime: "I will aspire to the unseen" he opined, swiftly narrowing his vocational path to that of poet or priest: "Love is perfected by the transition to the land of otherwhere" he was to write, "the land of dreams and fancies, where poets live whilst on earth." Attempts were made to suppress the volume by Johnson's ultra-conservative family.

Lionel Johnson was an ascetic aesthete, chasing after the misty wings of angels, venerating incensed air: "I feel as all must feel who believe in spirituality, an intense love of beauty in all its forms". (*Letters*) Though we may now consider the role of poet and priest to be quite different, there was a time when art was considered an expression of spiritual rapture. Responding to one of his friends Lionel was virtually forced to reveal a more corporeal aspect: "To come to earthly matters, I do take a great deal of exercise… I am a member of the Shakespeare Society and take leading female characters. I go out every day and declaim my part of the Twyford Downs."

A college photograph does nothing to dispel Lionel's other-worldly image. Enveloped in the voluminous folds of the traditional Winchester garb, he has a cut glass quality, like a finely crafted figurine that sets him apart from his larger, more mundane cohorts. Fellow pupil, Herbert Fisher, was to remember Johnson as:

> a diminutive, ethereal creature with a pallid beautiful face, an omnivorous reader, quite remote from the ordinary interests of the school and indeed contemptuous of them, but passionately enamoured of the beauties of Winchester. A certain aura surrounded him for he was rumoured to be a Buddhist, to have read all the books in the school library, and to drink *eau de cologne* for his amusement.

Although it has been alleged that a doctor later prescribed alcohol as a cure for Lionel's habitual insomnia, no medical man in their right mind would have suggested 80% proof *eau de cologne*, Victorian scent having a high spirit content. Sixteen and nipping for kicks suggests a worrying predisposition to alcohol. Lionel's interest in Buddhism soon abated, not least because the school alerted Captain Johnson to the young scholar's errant spirituality. Even worse, he shirked chapel for two days in a row, "A flagrant enormity in my eyes", Lionel was to confess to a friend.

Forever at odds with sleep, Johnson took to nightly wanderings, which inspired not just his poetry but his moonlit, sepulchral sensibility. In the silent cloisters he jotted down the epitaphs of pupils who had faded too soon from life: "here sleeps George Flower: O fair and early flower! But oh! The sooner was that flower to fade. Poor fourteen years a Fellow he: with power, Death's footstep called him hence;

and he obeyed." Lionel Johnson came of age when the art of mourning was at its peak, Queen Victoria having ignited an elaborate death cult following Prince Albert's departure in December 1861. As the bells tolled for her Prince a fine black veil descended across England that would take nearly forty years to lift. Never had the funereal been so fashionable or so elegantly accentuated.

A melancholy, sensitive soul, Johnson was thus a perfect candidate for a heightened sense of poetic morbidity: "Perhaps Death is the well of life?" he pondered, finding light in the darkness. "Then I can look forward for Death." (*Some Winchester Letters*) Winchester ran amok with ancient spirits and Johnson attempted to commune with them. Alone he ventured out, candle in hand down cobbled walks, under arches, into the dismal, moss covered domains of the dead whilst his friends, untroubled companions to rest, slept easy. But not Lionel:

> I have often gone into churchyards, and even when possible vaults and charnel houses, to try and hear the truth from the lips of spirits, to force the paraphernalia of death to unfold their secret: I have tried, oh, so earnestly tried, in utter faith to make the dead hear me, feel for me, comfort me. But the dead are deaf, or else too happy to listen. Don't think me mad: I am only human. You see, I know that there is a truth somewhere: I will not accept it as a creed of churches or philosophies. I will find it for myself.

In spite of his nightly vigils, Lionel was not one to shirk and by 1884, he had attained the level of prefect in both the chapel and as a senior. He also joined the School Mission Committee which he seemed to have enjoyed immensely: "Sunday classes, talks with boys of 18, ritualistic adorabalities: clubs, vespers, teas." (*Letters*) Most importantly, Johnson began editing the school paper, transforming *The Wykehamist* from a sporty rag into a literary journal. Rather than the usual match scores, the paper's cricket aficionados would have been perplexed to find a poem by Johnson dedicated to Baudelaire entitled 'Light! For The Stars Are Pale'.

Lionel who had once pondered "Why do people talk interminably about cricket?" pressed onwards in praise of Baudelaire, heedless of any criticism; "Darkling we dwindle deathward, and our dying sight strains back to pierce the living gloom." He also became an adherent of Walt Whitman as a letter to another pal, Edgar Jepson, attests:

> The flowers of evil are more beautiful than the sensitive plants of purity – and tears and protestations have an ugliness about them. Baudelaire, the lonely gardener of what Whitman calls 'intoxicating exotics', was also not far from the kingdom of Catholic ritual – a fact worthy of remembrance. Exquisite emotions and desires and pangs – these are the spirit of the best life possible. I find pleasure in my personal discontent – the desire for new pleasures is what keeps the life of me from dullness.

However, it was not as a budding poet but as a senior prefect that Lionel was to accompany a boy three years younger than himself to the headmaster's office so that he might be birched for a misdemeanour. Whilst Lord Alfred Douglas would do his best to forget the incident, it was to prove a continued source of amusement to Lionel in the years ahead. Sharing an abiding appreciation of Shakespeare as well as literary ambitions, they became firm friends and probably more. If we are to "pierce the living gloom" of the past, there are two Lionel Johnsons: "The little Saint" who according to Francis Russell "loved his fellow creatures in theory but found it difficult in the flesh" and "Giton" who in Dr. Iain Fletcher's words was "one of the leaders in a homosexual circle" in the last two years at Winchester.

Lionel's tragedy was not just the century in which he lived but his fear of intimacy. Johnson was never to be the athletic, confident type like his aristocrat pal, Lord Alfred Douglas, who went by the pretty soubriquet of Bosie. If Johnson was the Moon, pale and spectral, Bosie was the Sun, a gregarious golden boy with hair the colour of honey.

In Lionel's seventeenth summer, the family decamped to a grandly decaying mansion at Rhual in North Wales. The teenager's description of the journey demonstrates his lambent precocity:

We sped to Mold. Sparkling converse of the higher kind being impossible. I bought *Wuthering Heights* and read with rapt eagerness. My father remarked, with a Christian elevation of tone, 'that's the book where they're always cursing everyone, isn't it? I read it long ago!' My mother in agitated accents – 'My dear!' After which intercourse of souls, silence until Chester. It was awesome. (Arthur W. Patrick, *Lionel Johnson*)

The Rhual property had been in the family for some years, courtesy of Lionel's paternal grandmother, Lady Johnson. When in residence, the Captain and his wife participated in community life whilst Isabella's floral decorations graced the Church in Gwernaffield and she was called upon to hand out prizes at the local school.

Lionel appears to have absented himself from social events, according to reports in the *North Wales Chronicle*. Preferring his own company, he happily "walked himself to death" (*Letters*) in the neighbouring valleys. The untamed Welsh countryside awakened a sense of Celtic wonder which Lionel was to define as "a natural magic of emotion and soul." (*Post-Liminium*) Breathtaking scenery aside, it was a largely unremarkable summer until the arrival of a book by Walt Whitman: "He was almost thrown at me with a remark in Welsh by the Welsh postmaster as I walked through Mold, where a primitive cattle market was rampant." (*Letters*)

Lionel read Whitman aloud as he strolled through the village to the "accompaniment of bellowing beasts and Welsh execrations." Johnson's own literary ambitions over the holidays were devoted to an "intensely wretched and hopeless" play entitled *Miserabilia*. Lionel knew his "ferocious tragedy" would fail before he even posted it to the publisher, Charles Kegan Paul, and yet it was important for him to test his creative aspirations, admitting modestly "I have read worse." And so had the publisher who rejected *Miserabilia* in the nicest terms possible. Johnson was not unduly concerned as more pressing matters lay ahead.

The autumn, mild and golden, was less rhymed than usual as Lionel returned to Winchester and attempted to buckle down for the next stage of his education. Despite having attained an impressive scholastic record, all of his awards, including two gold medals for verse in 1885 and 1886, were of a literary nature. Johnson won a scholarship to New College, Oxford, only to repeatedly fail the university entrance exam due to a pronounced mathematical ineptitude. His family being held in high regard, the academic authorities put the boy out of his misery after a third sorry attempt and waved him on to Oxford, regardless.

Johnson's strangely youthful appearance and courtly profundity gave him an immediate mystique at Oxford. Fellow student, Campbell Dodgson, sets the scene:

It was whispered that he was the catechumen of strange religious rites which he celebrated in his rooms and that finding night and perambulation the only sure provocatives of thought, he was in the habit of letting himself out of College in the small hours.

Lionel used the darkness as he had done at Winchester, but seeking out night's haunted chapels wasn't always the safest of preoccupations: "climbing over gates or walls after hours… If I live to be Pope, I shall carry the mark of that sin upon me; a scar on my wrist, which was run through by a spike upon the wall." (*Letters of Louise Imogen Guiney*, 1926) Johnson's habitual lack of sleep may also have left him disorientated, exacerbating a tendency to drift off into silences by the afternoon, as observed by Lord Alfred Douglas.

The lack of a clearly delineated state of being, or indeed of a single philosophy to which Lionel might have safely anchored himself, was identified by the philosopher George Santayana, who visited him at Oxford in April 1887. Santayana was to find Lionel in his rooms, at the furthermost point of one of the New College buildings. Johnson's chambers overlooked a park, the peaks of trees brushing the skyline. Scanning the horizon, George imagined Lionel filling the empty sky with poetry and found him in a pensive mood: "Pointing to the distant horizon Lionel Johnson said sadly: 'Everything above that line is right, everything below it is wrong.'"

Like a set piece from a stage production of life, a central table in the main room of Lionel's chambers featured a jug of Glengarry whisky placed between two open books, Baudelaire's *The Flowers of Evil* and Whitman's *Leaves of Grass*. Under the watchful gaze of portraits of Cardinal Newman and Cardinal Wiseman, Johnson expounded to his Spanish guest upon his

Celtic kinship, Catholic conversion, whether to become a monk or a priest but always a poet. It was Santayana who first wrote of Lionel's propensity for merging truth with fiction, yet praised him as a mystic:

> I returned often, and should have gladly grown old in that atmosphere, yet not in order to indulge the impulse to dream awake: rather in order to remove the pressure of reality. (*Middle Span*, George Santayana, Constable & Co, 1947)

Unfortunately, George missed the unveiling of two illustrations by Simeon Solomon, a depiction of Sleep as a young man and a portrait of Emperor Hadrian's beloved Antinous, the latter described by Lionel as "The very incarnation of a beautiful and probably vicious youth." Once a prominent artist lauded by the Pre-Raphaelites, Simeon Solomon had been ostracised by the mainstream art establishment following his arrest and trial for homosexual soliciting in 1873, though his work continued to be collected privately, Oscar Wilde being an admirer. The extravagant loveliness of Simeon's pictures provided a dreamscape for the normally ascetic Johnson, who subsisted on eggs, tea, cigarettes and, when in the mood, lengthy walks, which he was to continue on a reading break in Devon in August, 1888.

Beguiled by nature and spirits of the air, Lionel penned 'A Cornish Night', his own bloom as frail as the white flowers of sea spray that so entranced him. Inevitably, at every inn he stopped off at on his walking tours, a motherly landlady would gently chastise him for playing truant. Lionel quite revelled in the mischief of the situation, as Johnson's American friend, Louise Imogen Guiney, was to recall:

His extreme sense of humour forbade annoyance over the episodes; rather was it not unwelcome to one who had no hold on time, and was as elemental as foam or air. (Obituary, *Catholic News*)

At Oxford, Johnson had started drinking alone in his room, the ever present jug of whisky a seemingly benign reminder of doctor's orders. If those rumours of "strange rites" were anything to go by, he may also have experimented with hashish in the company of Ernest Dowson, the unfortunate, if poetically gifted, son of consumptives. Both students had a predisposition to altered states, Ernest having taken to alcohol with the same alacrity as Lionel. However, Johnson's nocturnal habits began to catch up with him as a stern letter from the New College warden, sent shortly before he was due to take an examination in 'Greats', bears out:

I hope you are feeling tolerably well and will ensure such means as you can to ensure your being up in time and such self-mastery as you can to enable you to go through with the examination. If you can only do yourself justice I shall have good hopes for the result. I have been grieved and vexed this term that you have not been able to shake yourself free from your slack, invalid ways as I feel sure they have not been for your good.

A daring essay on Petronius, the author of *The Satyricon*, had already cost Johnson a first in Classical Moderations, but it didn't cost him the support of one of Oxford's most influential dons, Walter Pater, whose historical novel *Marius The Epicurean* had brought him wide acclaim. When Oscar Wilde visited Pater in Oxford, the distinguished teacher recommended Lionel to him. The nervous anxieties that prevented Lionel from sleeping, that affected his moods and led him to drink, fared better committed to poetry than weighing upon his soul. In youth's prime and on the threshold of what should have been a promising future, Lionel was filled with the terrible foreboding chronicled in his most prophetic poem. 'Mystic and Cavalier' was to prove chillingly apt from the opening line: "Go from me: I am one of those who fall" to its sorrowful conclusion.

Whatever tore at him in solitude made Johnson a poet of conviction, worthy of the esteemed Pater's respect and friendship. Oscar Wilde, who enjoyed cultivating the talent of younger men, promptly dropped Lionel a note. Even though it was lunchtime, Johnson was to be found dozing under a mountain of books. Tousle haired and barely awake, he grabbed his cigarettes and hurried out to greet the renowned author. Wilde's story 'The Picture of Dorian Gray' had caused a recent sensation when it had been serialised in *Lippincott's Monthly Magazine*, garnering praise and damnation. *The Daily Chronicle* had decried Dorian as "…a gloating study of the mental and physical corruption of a fresh, fair and golden youth."

Recalling meeting the "divine Oscar" for the first time, Lionel's usual affected urbanity slipped to show him as an awed 22 year old: "I found him delightful" he enthused to his friend, Arthur Galton, continuing "He discoursed with infinite flippancy, of everyone... laughed at Pater and consumed all my cigarettes. I am in love with him." Oscar was to respond with equal enthusiasm: "I hope you will let me know when you are in town. I like your poetry – the little I have seen of it – so much, that I want to know the poet as well."

Johnson began exploring London life as Oscar was putting the finishing touches to the book-length version of *Dorian Gray* but it didn't mean that Wilde couldn't come out to play. Wilde resided in Tite Street, Chelsea, with his wife, Constance, and their two young sons, Cyril and Vyvyan. Like

Dorian, his foremost literary creation, Oscar was already living a parallel existence, having commenced an affair with the critic, Robbie Ross, whom Johnson had met in Oxford and deemed "delightful."

In his book *The Middle Span*, George Santayana claimed that two years at Oxford had given Johnson an aptitude for banter, but it would depend on which Lionel you encountered. "Pious" Lionel perceived the city as if it were Blake's Jerusalem, albeit with a few unwittingly decadent flourishes: "London is chilly and I haunt warm incensed churches; the priests have beautiful gold vestments, the altar is lilied; the whole thing gently soothes." To aspiring poet Richard Le Gallienne, "uncomplicated" Lionel claimed to like "whisky, dogs, the Alhambra and a joke." "Social" Lionel had always found camaraderie in groups and was introduced to Herbert Horne of the Century Guild Circle by Arthur Galton.

Initiated by Horne, architect, Arthur Mackmurdo, and illustrator, Selwyn Image, the Guild was a William Morris-inspired design collective with its own magazine, *The Century Guild Hobby Horse*. Beyond school publications, *The Hobby Horse* was the first professional journal to feature Lionel's work, including the homoerotic poem 'A Dream of Youth', which he dedicated to Lord Alfred Douglas. A beautifully designed imprint, *The Hobby Horse* also boasted contributions from Oscar Wilde and Ernest Dowson. The Guild's founder, Herbert Horne, was another of Simeon Solomon's patrons, drawing together the tapestry of Lionel's life. The penalties for male to male relationships were unthinkably harsh, as the fate of Simeon Solomon demonstrated. Although he evaded imprisonment, beyond a few patrons, Solomon was socially excommunicated, exacerbating a tendency to drink. The Royal Academy never exhibited his work again and the gifted Simeon ended his days as a destitute pavement artist.

In the introduction to *Sexual Heretics – Male Homosexuality in English Literature from 1850-1900*, (Routledge and Keagan Paul, 1970) Brian Reade summarises the prevailing atmosphere Lionel and his friends endured, describing it as "curiously inconsistent half-tolerant, half-hostile." It was under these auspices that Johnson began frequenting the Crown pub on Charing Cross Road, becoming a denizen of the "queer half world", a term coined by Iain Fletcher.

Author Rupert Croft-Cooke, who was a later-in-life friend of Lord Alfred Douglas, alludes to Johnson and Wilde meeting at the Crown in his 1963 biography, *Bosie*, and describes the pub in *The Unrecorded Life of Oscar Wilde* (1972):

> The Crown was then the sort of pub frequented by vociferous young writers and a good many literary charlatans, painters and would-be painters, together with male prostitutes and servicemen looking for an addition to their miserable wages from one or another of the richer and older customers. It was not by any means exclusively a 'queer' pub, but having once gained a reputation for being lively, it was used by those who wanted to find a young sailor or an out-of-work stable boy, as well as by artists who may have been scarcely conscious of these activities... young men like Dowson, who had nothing in common with the male prostitutes, still came frequently.

Unfortunately, Rupert Croft-Cooke was rarely able to corroborate information. Johnson, who favoured the expression "Respectability is the best policy" and was the epitome of discretion, nevertheless did leave some subtle clues behind. The majority of his poems carry dedications, including the very lovely 'Bagley Wood', which is for William Percy Addleshaw.

In the textual notes to *The Complete Poems of Lionel Johnson* Dr Iain Fletcher comments: "William Percy Addleshaw was an Oxford Contemporary and an habitué of The Crown in Charing Cross Road" whilst Bagley Wood is a rendezvous spot in A.W. Clarke's gay coming of age novel *Jaspar Tristram* (1899).

Oxford may have begun to seem a little provincial in comparison to London, although the arrival of Lord Alfred Douglas in Lionel's final year would have been more than a balm. Bosie was one of the few prepared to discourse with Johnson through the night, as the young aristocrat was to recall: "He (Lionel) had a mania for not going to bed, and if he could get anyone to sit up with him he would discourse in the most brilliant manner way up till five o'clock in the morning." (*Lord Alfred Douglas The Autobiography*, Martin Secker, 1913)

In spite of distractions, Lionel left Oxford with First class honours. Barely had he graduated however, when he palled up with Ernest Dowson. For the first time, Johnson was free from either parental or academic restraint. London offered a dangerous liberation and Dowson was to prove a perfect drinking partner. As Ernest was to summarise in 'Carthusians':

We fling up flowers and laugh, we laugh across the wine
With wine we dull our souls and careful strains of art
Our cups are polished skulls round which the roses twine

Condemned to drain every night to the dregs and every bottle to the last drop, they would stay up drinking absinthe, stopping only to go to Morning Mass. Ernest, like Lionel, talked of entering a monastery and both were devoted to the idea of Catholic conversion. W.B. Yeats would come to describe them as "tragic penitents." However, whilst still young and at the beginning of their literary lives, there was an element of romance to their escapades, for were they not doing what was expected of poets? But not what was expected of priests, an ambition that Lionel seems to have retracted prior to taking up permanent residence in London.

By now a member of *The Hobby Horse* editorial team, Lionel moved into the Fitzroy Settlement home of the Century Guild Circle at 20 Fitzroy Street. A harbour of aesthetic refinement, Johnson shared the premises with Herbert Horne, Arthur Mackmurdo and Selwyn Image, with their domestic needs met by a Swiss manservant. Once again, Lionel chose rooms in the uppermost part of the house. The Fitzroy Settlement was an ideal situation as not only did it replicate the cloistered all-male environment that he was used to but it also placed Lionel within a creative setting, comprising of studios and a performance space for musical renditions and poetry readings, the mood enhanced by incense, frankincense and myrrh wafting through the fine Georgian house.

But change was in the air; "I do not prophesy long life to *The Hobby Horse*" Lionel was to pronounce. After nearly a decade in print, the house journal was in a state of flux; senior contributor Arthur Galton being opposed to articles of a decadent or symbolist nature appearing in the magazine. Whilst Lionel didn't agree with Galton, who was considerably older, Johnson wasn't sympathetic to the decadents, either.

In 1891, he dipped his sword in ink to pen 'The Cultured Faun' for the *Anti-Jacobin*, lampooning the "elaborate disorder"' and "sublime lunacy" of foppish dilettantes who paraded as decadents. "I heartily hate the cant of 'art for art's sake", Lionel was to vehemently proclaim during a lecture in Dublin in 1893, continuing, "I have spent years trying to understand what is meant by that imebecile phrase." W.B. Yeats, who accompanied Johnson to Ireland, would almost certainly have agreed. Art for both men was borne out of a desire for mystical transcendence rather than the concept of exquisite surface extolled by Oscar Wilde and his decadent acolytes. However, Johnson's unobtrusive despair, morbid inclinations and impassioned attachment to Catholicism – described by Yeats as a "virginal ecstasy" – coupled with a taste for absinthe made him a decadent by default.

Seized by the unnerving "conviction that the world was a bundle of fragments", (*Autobiographies*, Macmillan, 1926) a theme he would expand upon in the apocalyptic poem, 'The Second Coming', W.B. Yeats embarked on a two-fold quest. Hoping to reawaken the collective memory of his fellow countrymen and women, Yeats had begun collating Irish folk and fairy lore, a project encouraged by the author and editor Ernest Rhys. The great poets of Ancient Ireland had formed Bardic associations but there was no such alliance between the versifiers of London, W.B. confessing to Rhys: "I am growing jealous of other poets and we will all grow jealous of each other unless we know each other and so feel a share in each other's triumph." Of Welsh heritage, Rhys participated in Yeats' Celtic inclination and felt that Lionel Johnson would be sympathetic to their cause.

So it was that W.B. Yeats called at the Fitzroy Settlement and in the room closest to the stars encountered the man who would be his sage and theologian for as long as Johnson was able to disguise the extent of his drinking. "From the first, I devoted myself to Lionel Johnson", Yeats declared in *Autobiographies*.

> He had the delicate strong features of a head of a Greek athlete in the British Museum...and that resemblance seemed symbolic of the austere nobility of his verse... the external finish, the clearly marked lineaments of his body which seemed but to express the clarity of his mind.

In private, Lionel would refer to Yeats as 'The Faun from Sligo', a rather charming and apt description. (Letter to Louise Imogen Guiney, 1897) Yeats appeared to Lionel as if by a poetic summoning: "Yeats is a poet of prodigious beauty, whom I worshipped long before we were friends. But he and I are both Irish and his Celtic accent appeals to me." (Letter to Henry Davray) Yeats' endorsement enabled Lionel to shed the last vestiges of his Anglican, Tory background and he adopted Ireland as his spiritual home. Johnson's relationship with the truth sometimes had an elastic quality – hence if W.B. believed in Lionel's Celtic ancestry, it must be so. Consequently, Lionel briefly feigned a purring Irish brogue, addressing people as "me deearr." Whatever his eccentricities, they were forgiven by the Sligo Faun who had only recently attempted to raise the ghost of a flower by following seventeenth century instructions.

As 1890 drew to a close, Lionel returned to King's Mead for Christmas. It had been a decisive year, yet all he could think about was absinthe's opalescent allure, which prompted a letter to Dowson. The only consolation over the festive period was Joan, the family's pet dachshund, who was affectionately caricatured by Lionel: "She has no morals and her manners are uncertain." Johnson yearned for London and *la sorcière glauque*. Author Robert Sherard, who would see Ernest through his painful last hours, noted of absinthe: "It is an insidious drink, and the habit of consuming it grows upon its victim, who sooner or later has to abdicate all willpower in the control of his passion."

Back in London, Ernest Dowson was enlisted into Yeats' newly-formed poetic fraternity The Rhymer's Club. The group of twelve poets met at least once a week, usually but not exclusively at the Cheshire Cheese tavern in Fleet Street. After a dinner consisting of the tavern's famed lark-and-kidney pie they would retire to an upper room, order more punch or ale, smoke churchwarden pipes, recite their poems, then critique each other's work. Their best pieces they planned to publish in a yearly Rhymer's Club book. Yeats was opposed to "impurities" or generalities finding their way into poems, whilst a fining system was in place for anyone dropping a (decadent) lily into a sonnet. When Ernest Dowson was not up to reading his verses in public, Lionel stepped into the breach. Notes of each meeting were kept, although the person who described Lionel's reading voice as being "like a mouse's recitative" went unnamed. Johnson's critical silences however, had "beak and claws" according to W.B. Yeats.

In his excellent book, *The Rhymers' Club* (St. Martin's Press, 1994), Norman Alford points out the incongruity of such delicate beings as Dowson and Johnson supping ale and smoking unwieldly rustic pipes. Lionel rattled off a hearty tribute entitled 'At the Cheshire Cheese': "As we sit in good fellowship trusty and tried ." that has no relation to the angst beneath. The best of the Rhymers, Yeats, Johnson, Dowson and Arthur Symons, were all in their early twenties, their youth placing them at the forefront of new poetic expression. Symons captured the glittering artifice of London's night life whilst Ernest Dowson most famously cried for "Madder music and stronger wine" in 'Cynara', his poem of epic regret. (Lionel felt that 'Cynara' cried for a libation of cyanide according to *A Study in Yellow* by Katherine Lyon Mix. [The Greenwood Press, 1969])

In previous decades, poets had hymned the beauty of the countryside but these *fin de siècle* versifiers found inspiration in the city. Even Lionel turned briefly away from the elements for 'By the Statue of King Charles at Charing Cross', though the poem utilises his flair for sombre, brooding atmospherics. Divorced from English culture, Yeats heralded the Irish literary revival via the Rhymers, his 'Rose' poems steeped in Celtic mythology.

At 25, Richard Le Gallienne was the group's fashionable gadabout. Private notes reveal that the chivalrous Johnson, who would never have knowingly insulted anyone, found Richard "very irritating." This may have had something to do with their first meeting, when Le Gallienne assumed that Johnson was the son of one of the assembled Rhymers; "Fresh from provincial Liverpool, how was I to know?" was his excuse. However, he was to enjoy Lionel's hospitality on at least one memorable occasion when Ernest Dowson had swanned off to Soho. Despite Johnson's well-meant but ineffectual interventions, Ernest Dowson had become utterly obsessed with Adelaide "Missie" Foltinowicz, a pretty twelve year old whose parents owned a modest Soho eatery. The best one can say of Ernest's unfortunate rapture over "Missie" is that it belonged to the spirit not the flesh.

With Dowson otherwise embroiled, Richard Le Gallienne eagerly accepted Lionel Johnson's invitation to sample the "devil in a bottle".

> Absinthe! I had just heard of it, as a drink mysteriously sophisticated and even Satanic. It had the sound of hellebore or mandragora... It was spoken of with a self-conscious sense of one's being desperately wicked, suggesting diabolism and nameless iniquity. Did not Paul Verlaine drink it all the time in Paris? – and Oscar Wilde and his cronies at the Café Royal? (*The Romantic 90s,* Putnam and Company, 1951)

With his love of ritual, mastering the preparation of absinthe would have greatly appealed to Lionel. However, he was particularly vulnerable to the spirit's affect as Le Gallienne observed: "As I looked at his almost diaphanous frame, I could not help even then thinking that absinthe was too fierce a potion for one so delicately made." Yet for all the risks, there were also gains, especially for those of a creative disposition as Richard reasoned:

Probably Johnson had been tempted to risk that dangerous experimentation with alcohol, particularly in the form of his favourite absinthe... it has for a time so quickening and clarifying an effect on the intellectual and imaginative faculties. But he was weak of body and the thing stronger than he.

Lionel Johnson's period of grace, 1891-1895, was brief, but he was to accomplish much. As he had written in 'Mystic and Cavalier': "the end is set: Though the end be not yet." Whilst an undergraduate, he had accrued debts with a book dealer. Although Lionel received an allowance from his family, he sought to pay his bills independently and worked hard to clear them, contributing features to a number of publications including *The Anti-Jacobin*, *The Pall Mall Gazette*, *The Daily Chronicle* and *The Academy*. His choice of journalism as a profession – and poet as a vocation – was a humble one for a man of his social pedigree who at the very least would have been expected to become the editor of a leading journal. However, Lionel Johnson was a retiring creature – "one should be quite unnoticeable" was another of his favoured expressions.

The eternal youth stopped having his photograph taken once he left university and politely declined to have his portrait painted by the accomplished society artist, William Rothenstein. On a happier note, it was Rothenstein who introduced Aubrey Beardsley to the younger contingent of the Rhymers. (*Aubrey Beardsley - A Biography*, Matthew Sturgis, Harper Collins, 1996)

There are those who doubt the tragic element of the *fin de siècle*, but the day-lilies, such as Beardsley, Johnson and Dowson, had barely a decade each in which to leave their mark. Aubrey and Ernest were consumptives but Lionel's predicament was far more singular. How hard it must have been for him to watch friends mature and follow the normal stages of development, whilst he remained a delicate curio. As Louise Imogen Guiney noted:

> the only other Englishmen of letters so elfin-small and light was De Quincey. Few persons could readily believe Lionel Johnson's actual age. With his smooth hair and cheek, he passed for a slim undergrown boy of sixteen.

What force of will it must have taken for Lionel to speak with authority and project to an audience, yet he prevailed as W.B. Yeats recalled: "one never thought of his small stature when he spoke or read." (*Autobiographies*) Through Yeats, Lionel immersed himself in the Irish Literary Society to whom he gave the following stirring speech: "if we are to foster, encourage and develop Irish literature, and not least of all, Irish poetry, it must be with a wise generosity; in a finely national, not in a petty provincial, spirit." Lionel began travelling to Ireland with Yeats, delivering lectures. The country's unkempt charm, amiable society and a more noticeable religiosity greatly appealed to Johnson. Unfortunately, he also enthusiastically embraced Ireland's drinking culture, leading to frequent showings of what W.B. called Lionel's "impenitent face", when the diminutive poet yielded to alcoholic excess. It's a shame that Lionel didn't take heed of the concerned nun who reprimanded him for being up past his bedtime when he was due to give a talk at a Dublin Convent. "Do you know that I am twenty-six?" asked Lionel indignantly. "I don't care what age you are" replied the good nun, "you don't look it and you ought to be in bed, whether you're twenty-six or not." (*Memories*, Katharine Tynan, Everleigh Nash and Grayson, 1924)

Introduction

"Twelve Fleet street nightingales" was how the *Daily Chronicle* described The Rhymer's Club but some sang more prettily than others. In a letter to a friend, W.B. Yeats pronounced the second rung of his versifying brethren, Thomas Rolleston, Arthur Hillier, John Todhunter and George Greene, as "intolerably bad." Fortunately, however, there was enough talent in the ranks to make the Rhymer's Club worth fighting for, Yeats trying to keep poetry alive in an increasingly unsympathetic world.

Oscar Wilde, although never a member, deigned to grace them with his presence on the odd occasion. As the Cheshire Cheese was too bohemian for Oscar's sophisticated taste, Yeats asked him to a night at the Fitzroy Settlement, on January 29th, 1891. Resplendent in evening dress, Oscar arrived fashionably late, accompanied by the handsome poet, John Gray, who was rumoured to have inspired Dorian's surname. Lionel reported upon the evening in a letter to Campbell Dodgson: "we entertained the other night eighteen minor poets: from Oscar Wilde to Walter Crane, with Arthur Symons and Willie Yeats between. They all inflicted their poems on each other. Wilde is publishing Dorian Gray as a book, with additions that improve it... I have made great friends with the original of Dorian: one John Gray ...aged thirty with the face of fifteen."

Wilde presented Lionel with a signed advance copy of *The Picture of Dorian Gray*. In return, Lionel wrote some verses in Latin, dedicated to Wilde. 'In Honour of Dorian and his Creator', was not to be translated or published in Johnson's lifetime which one suspects is exactly how he wanted it to be. Iain Fletcher in his introduction to 'The Complete Poems', notes "Johnson's historical importance is due to his being the first competent English Latinist to revive Mediaeval stress and rhyme."

When in good shape, Lionel always supported his pals and remained highly enamoured of Oscar. Privately, however, he was ailing, as another letter written to Campbell Dodgson less than two weeks after the Wilde-Rhymer's soirée attests: "I have been in the depth of misery all through this weary autumn and insufferable winter. To begin with the venomous fogs have nearly blinded me, and oculists have tortured me to death." His hours were to become increasingly unsocial as Yeats was to discover when he called for Lionel at five in the evening only for the manservant to report that: "He is always up for dinner at seven." Yeats reported an intimation of admiration in the retainer's voice. Ernest Rhys, meanwhile, dropped by on the way to a Rhymer's meeting at nine to collect Johnson, only he was still not yet up. He knocked on Lionel's door and cautiously peered into the darkened chamber. From the well of blackness, Johnson whispered in exhausted tones that he was "too busy to go to the club."

In his study *The Selected Letters of Lionel Johnson* (Tregara Press 1988), Murray Pittock states:

> Johnson, always frail, became a victim of drink-related illness very early, and this period marked the beginning of drink's absolute power over him. His hypochondria, here and elsewhere seem like his excuses, a method of avoiding the problem.

Lionel rallied with the first breath of spring and went to stay with Bosie at Magdalen. By his own admission, Lord Alfred virtually devoured Lionel's copy of *The Picture of Dorian Gray*. A modest estimate has him reading it at least fourteen times, although not in one sitting. As Lionel bade farewell to a Dorian-empassioned Bosie, it was with the promise that he would arrange an introduction to Oscar.

True to his word, when the summer holidays came around and Lord Alfred was staying at his mother's house in swish Cadogan Place, Johnson went to call for him. The cherry blossom was in bloom and the pals in good spirits as they took a hansom cab to the Wilde residence. Douglas at 20 was a poet of no little ability but still a novice keen to meet Dorian's creator; Johnson meanwhile was the kind-hearted catalyst who enjoyed bringing his friends together. Oddly, his generosity of spirit and association with Bosie has given occasional cause for Lionel to be undermined. In the otherwise authoritative *Oscar's Books* (Vintage, 2009) Thomas Wright describes Johnson as a "prematurely aged... Pierrot-like homunculus." Yet Yeats during this period, and as a first hand witness, portrays Lionel as "determined and erect... beautifully made, his features cut in ivory."

In the "when Oscar met Bosie" scenario, retold countless times by a legion of Wilde biographers, Lionel is all too often an awkward stepping stone to be swiftly passed over. Surprisingly, *Oscar Wilde And The Black Douglas,* penned in 1949 by Lord Alfred's nephew and the journalist Percy Colson, gives Johnson a stark prominence at the introductory stage:

> Fate knocked at the door of 16 Tite Street, in the person of Lionel Johnson, old Wykehamist, poet, distinguished Oxonian and homosexual, bringing with him Lord Alfred Douglas. The meeting was a *coup de foudre* for Oscar and for Lord Alfred. Oscar was enchanted with Lord Alfred's youth and his extraordinary beauty. Lord Alfred was flattered at the great Oscar's evident admiration... how could they guess that they had taken the first step on the road to ruin?

In his introduction to *The Collected Poems of Lionel Johnson* Iain Fletcher comments: "in a private letter the late Percy Colson informed me that Alfred Douglas used to boast that he had slept with Johnson on a number of occasions." Certainly the arc of Lionel's descent was to intensify as the Wilde-Bosie alliance became ever more apparent. A "long, patient and strenuous siege" was how Wilde was to describe his wooing of the playboy aristocrat. Whether by accident or design, within weeks of Johnson having made the fateful introduction, he was received into the Catholic Church, on St Alban's day, June 22nd, 1891, at Saint Ethelreda's, Ely Place, London; the officiating priest, Fr. William Lockhart, an associate of Cardinal Newman.

Whilst Lionel was genuinely devout, Catholicism was the de-rigueur religion for decadents, appealing to the artistic imagination. Wilde even has Dorian Gray contemplating the Catholic Church: "the fuming censers, that the grave boys, in their lace and scarlet, tossed into the air like great gilt flowers, had their subtle fascination for him". Converts included Baudelaire, Huysmans and Verlaine, whilst in Lionel's circle, Walter Pater, Ernest Dowson, Aubrey Beardsley and Lord Alfred Douglas would all pledge themselves to the Church of Rome.

It is rarely the things that we hope to be remembered for that capture the imagination. Lionel's plan to write a book on *The Art of Thomas Hardy* began to take shape in 1891. It was a worthy project borne out of a need to consolidate his reputation as a serious author, but it was a far from inspirational choice. Struggling with alcoholism, Johnson was keen to present a sober, mature image. "No one must know there is anything wrong" should have been another of his sayings. With the summer's departure there is a sense of anti-climax or, to borrow a phrase from Hardy, "these slow blank months passed" until the death of Lionel's father, Captain William Victor Johnson, on September 16th, at the age of 69.

Three days after the funeral, Lionel wrote to Arthur

Galton, commending Wilde's skill in dealing with the anti-Dorian sentiments of "foolish critics", the salt not yet in the wound over Oscar's approbation of Lord Alfred Douglas. Before the year was over however, the statuesque Wilde had made a caricature of the diminutive Johnson, quipping that he had needed to "hail the first passing perambulator" when he'd staggered out of the Café Royal, drunk before lunch. Unfortunately, the "perambulator" quote was oft repeated. Oscar Wilde was not a cruel man and was probably being flippant. As Yeats pronounced of Wilde: "One took all his words for play." (*Autobiographies*) But the stage had become infinitely bigger and Oscar's words ever more valued as his fame grew, Yeats conceding: "he had turned his style to a parade and thought it was his show and he the Lord Mayor." The siege was over; Wilde had conquered, and Johnson was supplanted in Bosie's affections by Oscar.

Another who was ousted in the new dynamic was John Gray; the "Dorian" who never was eventually left London and became a priest. Some years after the deaths of Wilde and Johnson, Fr. John Gray came upon the first Rhymer's Club anthology amongst his possessions and made of it a present to Lady MacLagan, in February, 1906. Along with the volume, the priest sent a note; "I enclose you the book of the Rhymer's Club. It is an interesting relic of all that history. It only means little in respect of Dowson, Lionel Johnson and Yeats. The rest (excepting Arthur Symons) were preposterous." Lord Alfred Douglas meanwhile became Wilde's new poet elect and took over the editorship of an Oxford journal, *The Spirit Lamp*, to which Lionel would contribute, alongside Oscar, suggesting camaraderie; but it was on paper only. Aside from the odd stray such as the morbid and mysterious Count Stenbock, the majority of writers comprised the "Wilde Set", including Robbie Ross and the Crown crowd, featuring William Percy

Addleshaw. As Bosie's biographer Caspar Wintermans noted in his very fine account *Lord Alfred Douglas: A Poet's Life and His Finest Work* (Peter Owen, 2007): *The Spirit Lamp* "bore an 'aesthetic' signature; verses on Hylas, Ganymede and Hyacinthus, alternated with articles on Verlaine and Wilde."

"I have an arm-chair now, and live in it" Lionel was to write to Campbell Dodgson in December 1891, "so my delicate scripture will be more than commonly dark. Here I have been enlightening the world through the columns of some half dozen papers since October: very busy and rather ill: my doctor says grim things about spinal paralysis." Despite the gloomy prognosis, Lionel remained committed to his interests, as he told Campbell; "I have turned lecturer in general to all the Catholic societies in London… wild Protestants deny my statements, and insult my person: and in calming a controversial mob I have few equals."

In his quieter moments, Lionel acted as advisor to W.B. Yeats and his collaborator, Edwin Ellis, who were studying the prophetic writings of William Blake. Another tangential project was *Bits of Old Chelsea* which featured 41 etchings by Walter Burgess, complimented by text from Lionel and Richard Le Gallienne. Judging by Lionel's correspondence with his publisher, John Lane, *Bits of Old Chelsea* was not an edifying project, Le Gallienne keeping Johnson waiting around: "If you see him, curse him gently yet firmly for me, and insist upon his coming to talk this blessed Chelsea book over with me?" Richard, unlike Lionel, attended the first night of Wilde's play *Lady Windermere's Fan* at the St. James Theatre, on February 20th, 1892. Also present at the premiere were Lord Alfred Douglas, Aubrey Beardsley and Robbie Ross. Mrs Wilde was away at the sea-side with the children. The applause still ringing in his ears, Oscar returned to his home in Tite Street with Lord Alfred Douglas, initiating intimacies for the first time.

If these were Oscar's champagne days, they must have been as bitter as wormwood for Lionel Johnson. The proof of his ire and sorrow is to be found in 'The Destroyer of a Soul', written during this period and dedicated to Wilde. "It was one of the griefs of his later years that he had introduced me to Wilde" Douglas would comment in his 1913 *Autobiography*:

> this sonnet ('The Destroyer of a Soul') was written a year before the final catastrophe and Lionel Johnson's natural kindness of heart constrained him, in his sorrow for Wilde's terrible punishment, to deny the reference to Wilde of this sonnet to many people, though he admitted to me that he had meant it for Wilde at a time when he considered that he was ruining me, his junior by eighteen years.

After Lionel stayed with Bosie at Lady Queensberry's country residence in Salisbury, (*Bosie*, Rupert Croft Cooke, W.H. Allen, 1963) it was agreed that he would arrange for Campbell Dodgson to act as tutor to Lord Alfred. Although *The Spirit Lamp* was burning brightly, Bosie's studies were falling far behind his social life and his mother was apprehensive. Lionel's motives, however, were not entirely altruistic, as Campbell's appointment meant that he could keep an eye on the Bosie/ Wilde tryst from afar.

In 1893, W.B. Yeats dedicated *The Rose and other Poems* to Lionel Johnson. In spite of Lionel's gradual dissipation, he was still possessed of a charisma and intellectual verve that would make him both muse and associate to The Sligo Faun. Having completed *The Celtic Twilight*, W.B. embarked upon *The Secret Rose*, which he described as "weird stories from the middle ages in Ireland." (Interview with Katharine Tynan, *The Sketch*) Johnson haunts *The Secret Rose* as Owen Aherne, who has "lost his soul from looking out of the eyes of angels." *The Secret Rose* contains a mystical allegory entitled 'The Tables of The Law', wherein Owen's philosophy that "the beautiful arts were sent into the world to overthrow nations and finally life itself" mirrors the fiercely ideological side of Lionel, who had spent more time in books than being. One evening, in his neat little room, as Yeats was to recall, Lionel admitted: "You need ten years in a library, but I have need of ten years in the wilderness." (*Autobiographies*)

In September, Lionel and W.B. returned to Ireland where they stayed with Yeats' pal, Joseph Quinn, a homosexual medical student who wore make-up and women's apparel. Quinn had been involved in setting up the National Literary Society and it was hoped that a journal might evolve from it. Clearly, Yeats was comfortable in the company of gay men. The tragedy is that Lionel was loved, after a fashion, by Yeats and probably never knew it. In a letter written to the esteemed folklorist, Lady Gregory, following Johnson's demise, W.B. commented: "He (Lionel) had the subtle understanding of a woman and his thought flowed through life with my own, for many years, almost as if he had been one of the two or three women friends who are everything to me."

The Athenaeum, a well-respected literary journal, reviewed the second Rhymer's anthology on 25th August, 1894, singling out Johnson's 'To Morfydd'...as "the best thing in the whole book, with its curious haunting refrain." There is also a dark undertow in the offerings of those poets to whom Lionel was closest, especially Yeats' sinister 'The Folk of The Air' which makes a good companion for 'To Morfydd'. Ernest Dowson's contribution, 'Extreme Unction', was dedicated to Johnson, the poem taking its title from one of the last rites performed by a priest. The romantic years of Ernest and Lionel's drinking were long over, their roles as W.B. Yeats' "elegant tragic penitents" (*Autobiographies*) assured in the imagination of Ireland's greatest visionary.

Yeats, accompanied by his penitent muses, Johnson and Dowson, attended one of the most important literary soirées of the year; the launch party for *The Yellow Book* at the Hotel D'Italie, on Old Compton Street. *The Yellow Book*, published by John Lane, was to provide a stylish platform for art editor Aubrey Beardsley's illustrations whilst featuring the best writers of the era. The consumptive Aubrey was determined to make the most of it: "The doctors give me five years, but oh! Have a cigarette". The launch was a huge success, Lionel introducing his cousin, the writer Olivia Shakespear (née Tucker) to Yeats. Trapped in an unhappy marriage that had produced one child, Olivia confided in Lionel and remained the only family member to whom he had any emotional connection. The resemblance between them was striking, Olivia possessing the same refined features as her cousin. Unlike Lionel, however, Olivia had taken many lovers and was soon to begin a lengthy affair with W.B. "She felt and thought as he did" Yeats would later comment. (*W.B. Yeats A Life*, RF Foster, Oxford University Press, 1998)

Christmas coincided with the publication of *The Chameleon*, which was to gain notoriety in the impending Wilde court case. The creation of John Francis Bloxham, a student friend of Bosie's, the journal borrowed its subtitle, "A Bazaar of Dangerous and Smiling Chances", from a story by Robert Louis Stevenson. Intended for the homosexual connoisseur, *The Chameleon* picked up the torch lit by *The Spirit Lamp*. Brian Reade, in his preface to *Sexual Heretics*, noted:

1894 could be described as a golden year for homosexuals in England, for the very reason that it was the last year for a long time in which they could take shelter in public ignorance or tolerance to propagate a non-hostile climate of taste and opinion.

As well as featuring Lord Alfred's most well-known poem 'Two Loves' which contains the famous line: "I am the love that dare not speak its name", Oscar contributed 'Phrases and Philosophies For The Very Young.' Lionel rose to the occasion with the teasing essay 'On the Appreciation of Trifles', the church mouse unusually emboldened:

I am sure we must all constantly feel that we are under the deepest obligations to certain companies, and, strangely enough, to the Government officials connected with the Post Office, for filling our streets with the graceful, neatly uniformed figures of those that bear our messages and our telegrams.

Playing to the journal's readership, Johnson was alluding to the relatively recent Cleveland Street scandal, which centred on a male brothel where telegraph boys topped up their meagre earnings catering to upper class gentlemen. (Needless to say, a member of the royal family, Prince Albert Victor, was said to have been a frequent visitor, while a few gentlemen of high ranking office had to flee the country due to press exposure.)

On April 25th, 1895, Oscar Wilde was found guilty of committing acts of "gross indecency" and sentenced to two years hard labour. Bosie's father, the irascible Marquis of Queensberry, had gone after Wilde like a maddened hunting dog in pursuit of its prey, although it was Oscar who had ill-advisedly initiated court proceedings. Under provocation by the

Marquis, the playwright felt he had little choice. Queensberry also succeeded in ruining his son, Lord Alfred Douglas, by dint of association. Oscar's friends blamed Lord Alfred for the catastrophe that had befallen Wilde and the golden boy was forever tarnished.

Lionel Johnson blamed himself and on the day of the verdict was even more intoxicated than usual, according to Frances Winwar in *Oscar Wilde And The Yellow Nineties* (Harper & Brothers, 1940). For someone as private as Lionel Johnson, the court case was the stuff of nightmares. A note of disapproval is apparent in a letter, since lost, that Yeats recalled having received from Lionel. (*Autobiographies*) The punctuation is that of W.B., the contents ring true to Johnson's perception: Wilde had a "a cold scientific intellect"; he got a "sense of triumph and power, at every dinner table he dominated, from the knowledge that he was guilty of that sin which, more than any other possible to man, would turn all those people against him if they knew." Nonetheless, Yeats also notes that Lionel felt badly for Oscar, but not his imitators. By "imitators" Johnson may have been referring to none other than John Francis Bloxham, whose unfortunate story 'The Priest and The Acolyte' had brought *The Chameleon* into disrepute. The heinous tale of a priest who ravishes a fourteen-year-old and then encourages the boy to die with him has no grounds for defence.

In court, Oscar described Bloxham's tale as "bad and indecent" and claimed that he'd urged the editor to withdraw it. The damage was done, however, and Oscar blamed Bosie for dragging him into *The Chameleon* as well as into the dock in the damning prison epistle *De Profundis*. Characteristically, Lionel remained true to Lord Alfred and was one of the few to go and stay with him during his European exile, visiting him in Italy. Johnson also sent a letter imploring a mutual friend, More Adey, to encourage others to support Douglas, which concluded: "It is very important for Bosie's health and peace of mind, that he should be alone as little as possible... most of his Oxford friends seem unable or unwilling for various reasons to accompany him." (*Bosie,* Rupert Croft-Cooke.)

Oscar Wilde's incarceration marked the end of the decadent era: "The shadow of doubt fell on all with whom he had associated" wrote Katherine Lyon Mix in *A Study in Yellow* (Greenwood Press, 1969). Poor Aubrey Beardsley, whom *Punch* daubed "Awfully Weirdly", was asked to relinquish his position at *The Yellow Book*. He was devastated. The press had mistakenly reported that Oscar had a copy of *The Yellow Book* on his person when he was arrested. In fact it was a novel bound in yellow by Pierre Louys, entitled *Aphrodite*. Anything deemed unnatural or artificial was immediately suspicious, including Aubrey Beardsley. *The Yellow Book* without Aubrey was despondently grey.

Beardsley was to find comfort in the words of Father John Gray, but who was Lionel able to turn to for support? Sadly, 1895 marked the beginning of the end of his relationship with The Faun from Sligo. Inevitably, Johnson's intellectual vision, his capacity for clarity which Yeats had counted on, was becoming dimmed by drink. "I would urge him to put himself into an institute", W.B. was to comment:

> one day when I had been very urgent, he spoke of 'a craving that made every atom of his body cry out' and said the moment after, 'I do not want to be cured,' and a moment after that 'In ten years I shall be penniless and shabby, and borrow half-crowns from friends.' (*Autobiographies*)

Lionel assumed a better fate than the one that awaited him. However, he could not assume his way out of Arthur

Mackmurdo's terse command to leave the Fitzroy Settlement. It was the not the first or the second time that Lionel had taken a tipsy tumble down the stairs, lit candle in hand, when showing Ernest Dowson to the door after a particularly heavy drinking session. From Mackmurdo's perspective, however, it was to be the last time, the other tenants being concerned that Johnson might set the house ablaze. In 'Mystic and Cavalier' the fatal course is already set: "The clouds are breaking from the crystal ball/Breaking and clearing and I look to fall."

An exceptionally poignant written appeal to Mackmurdo failed, despite Lionel's best efforts: "I am exceedingly distressed by your letter", Johnson wrote back:

> though I fully recognise your just cause of complaint. But may I ask for a further trial, upon the condition that I take the pledge at once – which I should have done long ago – that upon giving the least disturbance I go. Also, I promise to have no drink in my rooms but for friends. As long as it depends on my own will, I am quite hopeless: but the pledge is different. I once took it temporarily, for a month and kept it rigidly: and should have taken it for good and all, but for falling ill. If you consent to this, it will be the greatest of many kindnesses. I can't tell you how sorry I should be to leave the house where I have lived for five years and had so many friends.

But it was to no avail and by September Lionel Johnson had removed to chambers at 7 Gray's Inn Square. "I have left my old quarters" Johnson would write to author Edmund Gosse, "and settled down in this old-world place of memories." His rooms looked out on to a leaf dappled lawn enabling a feigned contentment. But as The Faun from Sligo was to observe, the milk on the door-step was left to sour.

In *Autobiographies*, Yeats reflected on the exact moment when he realised the hopelessness of Johnson's situation. Overwhelmed by pressing concerns, W.B. called on Lionel for advice and found him at his desk:

> He seemed perfectly logical, though a little more confident and impassioned than usual... when he rose from his chair, took a step towards me in his eagerness, and fell on to the floor; and I saw that he was drunk. From then on, he began to lose control of his life.

Although Yeats now distanced himself from Lionel, he was to remain a melancholy presence in the Faun's "new/old Celtic mysticism." Both men contributed to *The Savoy*, the last great journal of the era. Edited by Arthur Symons, *The Savoy* had been intended as a pick-me-up for Aubrey Beardsley, who gladly took the role of art editor; but it would turn into a twelve month swan-song. Despite a greater maturity of contents, the first death blow was struck by those arbiters of taste, W.H. Smith the bookseller, who refused to stock it, just as they'd refused to stock *Dorian Gray*.

England was not about to forgive the flower of its finest creatives, who were now quite literally dying on the vine. Aubrey Beardsley's illustration 'Death of Pierrot' was a portent much like Ernest Dowson's sombre poem 'Epilogue', sent from Brittany where he now resided. Johnson contributed three religious sonnets that struggle in vain to reach the heights of old. At the time of their publication, he had retreated to King's Mead to escape the summer. A scribbled note to Charles Sayle sees lachrymose Lionel comparing Windsor Forest to "the tropics": "it's too hot to write, I am simply wasting away."

The Rhymer's Club faded out with the Decadent movement; the best of their members now established literary names. For

Yeats, it was time to move on. Mired in alcoholism, Lionel Johnson's muse had stalled, yet he was still able to charm new friends such as the American poet Louise Imogen Guiney. A literary Anglophile who would visit as often as her job as a postmistress allowed, Louise belonged to a tentative network of Catholic writers that included Katharine Tynan and her husband, Henry Hinkson.

Few were to understand Johnson's poetry quite so keenly as the cultivated Miss Guiney: "he had a homeless genius: it lacked affinity with the planetary influences under which he found himself here" or able to depict his enigmatic quality quite so well: "small and silent, with a knowing side-long smile, pleasant as a bookish fay's. He is not noticeably human…" They were to regularly correspond, the distance enabling Lionel to remain a romantic figment in their courtly exchanges: "I love to sleep under the stars" he wrote to Guiney on July 8th, 1897:

> with no roof between us: in Wales and Cornwall I have spent marvellous nights: one on Tintagel, when the souls of the Celtic knights were abroad on the sea-wind. But Edgon was terrible: purple vault above, purple plain around; the oldest loneliness in the world. I lay in the heather, dreading to wake…

Some weekends, Johnson would venture out to rural Ealing to stay with Tynan and her husband, arriving top-hat in hand, "all fine manners and courtesies." In the summer sheep-bells could still be heard from flocks grazing in nearby Perivale Fields. The winter paints a different picture according to Katherine:

> My outstanding memory is of Lionel coming in blue-lipped and frozen, one Sunday morning about ten o'clock, so I suppose it must have been winter again. He

refused breakfast but I can remember running for a glass of port wine which I had to hold to his lips, so excessively was he shivering. It brought life to him and he went off afterwards to Mass at St Benedict's. (*Memories.*)

There is a touch of melodrama to Iain Fletcher's sorrowful depiction of Lionel Johnson in *The Complete Poems*, unsteadily traversing the pubs of Holborn and Bloomsbury, supping with Irish conspirators by day and concluding with late night literary tipples with Ernest Rhys and Edgar Jepson, who was to portray Lionel in his *Memories of a Victorian* – drunk of course. Yet Lionel clung precariously on, steadied himself for work and produced the marvellous, self-mocking 'Incurable' for *The Pageant*. A mist shrouded depiction of a suicidal versifier; 'Incurable' also doffs its top-hat at Ernest Dowson and Arthur Symons.

As the end of the century loomed, "The moonstruck poet" amongst whose ranks Johnson recognised himself, was on the verge of extinction: "Suddenly the horror of a long life spent in following the will-o'-the-wisp, or in questing for Sangrails and Eldorados, fell upon him: he refused to become an elderly mooncalf." ('Incurable') *Ireland*, a second book of poems, which Johnson admitted was "hopelessly in the would-be austere and hieratic manner", was also published. The poet, like his verse, was starting to close in upon himself, the latest sonnets without flesh in their asceticism. "I like stern faces, austere and mortified" he wrote to Louise Imogen Guiney in July, 1897. Did they manifest the control that Lionel lacked?

Arthur Symons rarely wrote from an authentic perspective, his work a borrowed costume from the theatre of poetry in which he was immersed: "I do not think he (L.J.) ever got any pleasure out of drinking: he would sit up over night with absinthe and cigarettes in order to be awake to attend early Mass, but though his will was strong… the habit was stronger." Symons does however convey Johnson's peculiar resignation: "He seemed condemned to that form of suicide, without desire or choice in the matter."

A ghost before his time, Lionel began doing a last few sad rounds of goodbye, whilst he was still able. George Santayana, lecturing in metaphysics at Harvard but on vacation in London, was afforded a sorry last glimpse of his old friend at Francis Russell's rooms in Temple Gardens:

> He still looked very young, though he was thirty, but pale, haggard and trembling. He stood by the fireplace with a tall glass of whisky… and talked wildly of persecution. The police, he said, were after him everywhere. Detectives who pretended to be friends of his friend Murphy or of his friend, McLaughlin, had to be defied. Without a signed letter of introduction he could trust nobody. As he spoke he quivered with excitement, hatred and imagined terrors. He seemed to be living in a dream; and when at last he found his glass empty, it was with uncertainty that his hat sat on his head as with sudden determination he made for the door, and left us without saying good night. (*The Middle Span*)

At Christmas, Lionel declined an invitation from Victor Plarr to meet the poet, Emile Verhaeren, whose work he admired. He seems utterly lost, perplexed almost, as he responds to Victor: "I should have answered you before, but my movements have been so uncertain." His indefinite status was made official by his omission from a major study, *Living Poets of The Younger Generation*, by William Archer, in January 1898.

With his devoted mother and sister at his bedside, Aubrey Beardsley finally gave up his gallant fight for life on March

16th, 1898. A mere twenty-five years old, Aubrey died with a rosary entwined between his long graceful fingers and a copy of Dumas' *La Dame Aux Camélias* in his coffin. He was buried in Southern France, in the little town of Mentone where he had been staying for his health. The cemetery overlooked the Cathedral where Mass was said for his soul, a far simpler affair than the London requiem which took place at Farm Street Church in Mayfair, attended by "fashionable women and epicene men", as reported by Katherine Lyon Mix, who also described a down-at-heel Ernest Dowson as being "more like a lost soul than ever." Lionel added Beardsley's Requiem Mass to a growing list of events unattended: "I wish I could have been present" he wrote to Edmund Gosse on May 14th, 1898, offering no excuse for his absence although influenza had laid him low through the first few months of the year.

Unfortunately, whilst his manners were to remain impeccable, alcohol had begun to show on the former "angel visitant" and the Beardsley Mass would have drawn a sophisticated throng. Once so dapper, it was probably more than Lionel was up to. Katharine Tynan, who had lost contact with Johnson, was to report on his now unkempt appearance in *Memories*:

> My husband being in town one day met Lionel at some hostelry in Fleet Street. Lionel, looking rather dilapidated as to clothing but with the same air as the gentleman and the saint. He promised to come and stay with us… but he never came.

However, Lionel was able to do his bit for Aubrey from afar as he explained to Edmund Gosse:

> My most admired friend Miss Guiney, the poet and essayist, arranged with other Catholics to have a Mass

sung for Aubrey in a convent chapel at Boston: but none of them knew him well enough to give the officiating Jesuit father any material for an address: so she applied to me for a brief account of him in general, and in particular as a Catholic convert. I did my best.

Lionel managed a final trip to Dublin where he delivered a lecture on the poet James Clarence Mangan to the National Literary Society, on May 23rd, 1898. Johnson had an affinity with Mangan; a poetic rebel who lived in a dream world fuelled by alcohol and opium, with a weakness for literary hoaxes yet capable of writing glorious verse. Johnson's essay on Mangan, which appeared in *The Academy* just before he departed for Ireland, reveals as Iain Fletcher acknowledged: "considerable self-identification." Only by writing about another with similar predilections, could Lionel shed some light onto his own strange borderline existence:

It was a life of dreams and misery and madness, yet of a self-pity which does not disgust us and of weakness is innocent: it seems the haunted, enchanted life of one drifting through his days in a dream of other days and other worlds, golden and immortal, and with all this remoteness and his wretchedness, there was a certain grimly pathetic and humorous common-sense about him, which saved him from being too angelic a drunkard, too ethereal a vagabond.

And that is the mystery of Lionel Johnson transposed on to Mangan, both men "homesick for eternity". Johnson was not of this world, viewing it as "Maya" an illusion through which he was passing on the way to infinity. A diminutive changeling with an "elvish turn for a little innocent deception… he lived in a penumbra of haunting memories and apprehensions."

As 1898 bowed to winter, Lionel Johnson once again had cause to move, which would surely have added to an increasing sense of impermanence. He was slowly vanishing, though he put a brave face on it in a note to Thomas Hardy: "I have left the Inn of my Lord chancellor Bacon, the sinner, for that of my Lord Chancellor Moore the saint." (Feb 18th, 1899)

8 New Square, Lincoln's Inn, another prestigious, "old world" address, should have been the perfect abode for a retiring man of letters who kept odd, unsociable hours. Lionel's chambers, three sitting rooms and a bedroom, were annexed from the rest of house by a separate staircase and closed off from the world by a heavy oak door. By a stroke of luck, the apartment was splendidly secluded and the rent was remarkably low. During the day, the house was inhabited by lawyers who kept offices there. At night, aside from a caretaker who resided in the basement, Lionel should have been the only person in the upper part of the Georgian house, and perhaps he was, although it didn't always seem that way. The early nocturnal disturbances were too slight and too subtle to pin down as anything other than the workings of an old building after dark.

Lincoln's Inn is steeped in blood and history, several prominent and unusually ghastly executions having taken place in the nearby field. Up until the 17th Century, Lincoln's Inn Fields rivalled Tyburn for brutal, public dispatch. Few executions were as cruel as that of Mary Queen of Scots' co-conspirator, Lord Anthony Babington, who took his last tortured breaths on the sweet green lawns of Lincoln's Inn in 1586. Ordered to be hung but not unto death, he had to endure evisceration whilst still bearing a semblance of consciousness so that he might see his "privy parts" thrown onto a bonfire. A century later, Lord Russell, accused of treason, went to the chopping block where he encountered cack-handed executioner Jack Ketch. Despite having paid Ketch ten guineas to do the job swiftly, it took fumble-fingered Ketch at least five swings before Lord Russell expired. It is likely that the doomed Lord Russell was related to Lionel's friend, Francis, Earl Russell. No lesser than Charles Dickens, who had worked in a Lincoln's Inn legal office, mentioned a peculiar all-seasons mist that hung about the place, whilst *Bleak House* features a nefarious solicitor based there. Rumours also abounded that the lay-out of buildings duplicated the shape and measurements of the Great Pyramid. Lincoln's Inn was a forever autumn location and the centuries seemed to oppress the very air of that oddly-removed enclave in the city.

In his solitary quarters, Johnson was consuming two pints of whisky every twenty-four hours, according to Annie Jenkins, his laundress who had charred for him since the Fitzroy Settlement, and would give evidence at his inquest. Lionel had reached a staggering level of self-immolation, his delicate frame under continual siege.

How many people know the lonely? In Johnson's case, probably only Annie Jenkins saw him on a regular basis in those years of slow, inevitable fade. However, Lionel continued to meet with Lord Alfred Douglas, who had returned from European exile at the close of 1898. Via family connections to "Headquarters" – the legal establishment – Johnson had been able to ascertain that as long as Bosie didn't "play the fool again" he would be "running no risks." (Letter to Francis Russell, April 17th, 1899) In June, Lionel reviewed *The City of The Soul* for *The Outlook*, ensuring Lord Alfred Douglas at least one glowing write-up of his anonymously published collection of poetry. *The City of The Soul* did well until an emboldened Douglas put his name to a subsequent edition, thus ensuring a down-turn in sales, such was his infamy.

"One never saw peace more reposeful on features more ravaged" Robert Sherard was to write of Ernest Dowson who died aged 32, on February 23rd, 1900. Dowson's funeral at Ladywell Cemetery saw the last of the Victorian bohemians gather to mourn a literary wildflower. Ernest would surely have known that Lionel, alone in his room, would drink far more than he ought to, in memory of their fleeting days of wine and roses. Although Johnson's finest poems had all been written, 'Ash Wednesday', his tribute to Dowson, ranks amongst the better of his later offerings: "The visible vehement earth, remains to me; The visionary quiet land holds thee; But what shall separate such friends as we?" Poor Lionel, abandoned on oblivion's shores, as one by one, his friends departed before him. What better time for the poet's evil enchanter, 'The Dark Angel', to occupy his solitary delirium?

Written in 1893, Johnson's most famous poem is a harrowing abnegation of desire as he fights to save his soul from "The Master of Impieties". What Lionel was unable to verify was nonetheless intensifying, just like the poem: "Thou art the whisper in the gloom, the hinting tone, the haunting laugh..." Lionel's black-winged creature, his Dark Angel, was manifesting in his Lincoln's Inn chambers.

Whether the subject of delirium, drink induced psychosis, a prank or a genuine emanation, we will never know. Lionel Johnson was one who walked between worlds, his grasp of reality increasingly tenuous yet, as he was to discover, no one stayed in the chambers where he now resided, for long.

The poet discussed his concerns, in the strictest confidence, with an old friend, Ralph D. Blumenfeld, who was the News Editor of the *Daily Mail*. Lionel Johnson was a reserved soul so why turn to a journalist? Blumenfeld was a practical man, neither a sceptic nor a believer in the uncanny, who could be relied upon to investigate the allegations whilst keeping the poet's name out of the press. By the time the story broke in the *Mail*, under the headline "A London Ghost: Inexplicable Happenings in Old Chambers" on May 16th, 1901, Lionel Johnson had already fled the premises. Verifying Lionel's experience, Blumenfeld who wrote the piece anonymously, noted:

> My friend (LJ) filled up most of the wall space with books, read, wrote and mused during most of the day and part of the night, and he admitted to me in his more confidential moments that "things happened" there. He did not specify exactly what occurred, but after a time he became nervous and fidgety. Last month he left the chambers rather suddenly, declaring he could stand it no longer. He cleared away all his belongings, and once more the rooms were empty.

On Saturday, May 11th, Ralph accompanied by Max Pemberton, the editor of *Cassell's Magazine*, had spent the night in Lionel's former chambers and faced the dawn as shaken believers in a fiendish feathered entity. The evening had begun in typically journalistic fashion, notebooks and pencils at the ready. After conducting a thorough search of the premises to make sure they were alone, they scattered chalk dust on the floor, to record any movement or disturbance. Seated at the apartment's sole table, they began their vigil, Blumenfeld recalling: "We were both very wide awake, entirely calm, self-possessed and sober, expectant and receptive, and in no way excited or nervous. It was then about a quarter past midnight."

The next three hours passed in an unearthly sequence as door handles turned and latches clicked. Eventually, all of the doors in the apartment started to open and close of their own accord as if an invisible being was going from room to room. In total Ralph D. Blumenfeld recorded: "Four openings and three closings. The last openings took place at 2.7 and 2.9, and we both noticed marks on the chalk… the marks were clearly defined birds' footprints in the middle of the floor, three in the left-hand room and five in the right-hand room."

The story was to prove one of the last great supernatural mysteries of the Victorian age and the *Mail* was inundated with letters of inquiry and interest after publication. Even more curious is how the bewinged haunting, like everything Lionel touched, was doomed to a strange obscurity. Initially, the Society for Psychological Research promised to investigate, but there were several obstacles: the exact address was never given, Lionel wasn't identified and neither was Ralph D. Blumenfeld, because of his position as News Editor. Whilst this intensified the mystery, it made it impossible to follow through and the "Terrible true story of the bird elemental" as it was also known, eventually faded into the mist of Lincoln's Inn.

It cannot be coincidence that almost immediately after moving, this time to Clifford's Inn near Fleet Street, Lionel Johnson collapsed. He never even unpacked his beloved books, which had dwelled with him in lofty rooms at Oxford, lined his library at the Fitzroy Settlement, kept him company at Gray's Inn Square and had accompanied the poet to the doomed Lincoln's Inn abode. This time however, the books were to gather dust, like their owner.

Overwhelmed, Johnson was bed-ridden for close on eighteen months, the only witness to his pitiful state being Annie Jenkins, who would prepare his meals. His letters went not just unread but unopened, a matter of distress for his friends, including Louise Imogen Guiney: "It is to be feared that he was not properly nursed" she would write in the poet's obituary, "he had never known how to care for himself." No doctor was called – what medicine can cure a lack of love? 'The Precept of Silence' had always been Johnson's domain: "I know you: solitary griefs, Desolate passions, aching hours!"

Iain Fletcher gives the perfect summary: "the void that separates us from each other: that is Johnson's theme." Katharine Tynan had given up after finding the rooms at Lincoln's Inn locked. Lord Alfred Douglas, having run out of money, was trying to remake himself as a gigolo. Oscar Wilde had gone to a pauper's grave in the suburbs of Paris in November 1900. The dream that Lionel Johnson had once belonged to was over, a very lovely purple and gold pageant crushed by reality and the oncoming of a fearful new century not meant for one of such fine aesthetics.

Stirred by the oncoming spring of 1902, Johnson roused himself from the depths and responded to a letter from Lewis Hind, the editor of *The Academy*:

> You last wrote to me, some time, I think, in the last century, and I hadn't the grace to answer. But I was in the middle of a serious illness... during which I was not in the open air for even five minutes and hopelessly crippled in hands and feet. After that long spell of enforced idleness, I feel greedy for work.

But desire outweighed capability; something was very wrong, the porter of Clifford's Inn having to retrieve Johnson from the street, where he had collapsed.

There are numerous accounts of Lionel's last moments, Le Gallienne adding period detail for effect but not accuracy:

> he was to make that tragic end in Fleet Street, stupidly knocked down by a hansom cab, when, poor fellow, his good wits were not all, for the moment, at his service. A drunkard, in the ordinary sense, or even 'a drinking man,' Johnson was not and could never have been. (*The Romantic 90s*)

On September 29, an autumnal day of mist filtered sunshine, (Louise Imogen Guiney, Obituary, *Catholic News*) Annie Jenkins had checked on Johnson: "He looked very ill", she would tell the inquest. H.V. Nevinson, author of *Thomas Hardy* (1941), fancied that Johnson had fallen and cracked his skull on the corner of Fleet Street and Whitefriars, on the way to a meeting at *The Daily Chronicle*.

At nine in the evening, the spectral poet, perhaps hoping for some comfort or possibly even company, entered the Green Dragon pub in Fleet Street. The bar man, echoing Annie Jenkins earlier that same day, noticed how very ill Johnson looked. Like Jenkins, the bar man would also give evidence: "He went to sit in a chair and in trying to do so he fell slightly on his head."

The poet never regained consciousness and was taken to Saint Bartholomew's Hospital, where he died four days later. Katharine Tynan recorded that Johnson had died of a fractured skull, the poet's bone density being that of a child, but the autopsy revealed death due to a ruptured vessel. Lionel had been dying slowly as stroke followed stroke, like stars going out one by one. "Priests of a fearful sacrament!" he had exclaimed in the last verse of 'Mystic and Cavalier', "I come to make with you mine home." His friend, Fr. Dawson, administered 'Extreme Unction'.

On October 4th, 1902, the feast day of Saint Francis of Assisi, patron of saint of animals and nature, Lionel Johnson was released from life's illusion. He was buried at St. Mary's cemetery, Kensal Green, where he rests beneath a simple grey cross.

The poet of things forgotten, Lionel Johnson's ghost is said to haunt Lincoln's Inn, though his soul is surely with the angels.

Selected Bibliography

Books

Adams, Jad: *Madder Music, Stronger Wine,* I.B. Tauris, 2000

Alford, Norman: *The Rhymers' Club*, St. Martin's Press, 1994

Arnold, Matthew: *Poetry and Prose*, Oxford University Press, 1946

Blore, G.H. (ed): *Poems and Fragments by Wykehamists*, Private printing, 1938

Croft-Cooke, Rupert: *Bosie*, W.H. Allen, 1963

Croft-Cooke, Rupert: *Feasting with Panthers*, W.H. Allen, 1967

Croft-Cooke, Rupert: *The Unrecorded Life of Oscar Wilde*, W.H. Allen, 1972

Douglas, Lord Alfred: *Autobiography*, Martin Secker, 1929

Fletcher, Iain (ed): *Decadence and The 1890s*, Edward Arnold, 1979

R.F. Foster: *W.B. Yeats – A Life. Volumes 1&2*, Oxford University Press, 2003

Le Gallienne, Richard: *The Romantic '90s*, Putnam and Company, 1951

Johnson, Lionel: *The Art of Thomas Hardy*, Elkin Mathews and John Lane, 1894

Johnson, Lionel: *Some Winchester Letters*, Francis, Earl Russell (ed) George Allen and Unwin Ltd, 1919

Johnson, Lionel: *Complete Poems*, Iain Fletcher (ed) Unicorn Press, 1953

Johnson, Lionel: *Selected Letters*, Murray Pittock (ed) Tregara Press, 1988

Mix, Katherine Lyon: *A Study In Yellow*, Greenwood Press, 1969

Queensberry, The Marquess with Percy Colson: *Oscar Wilde and The Black Douglas*, Hutchinson & Co, 1949

Reade, Brian (ed): *Sexual Heretics*, Routledge and Keagan Paul, 1970
Sewell, Brocard: *In The Dorian Mode*, Tabb House, 1983
Sturgis, Matthew: *Aubrey Beardsley*, Harper Collins, 1998
Tynan, Katharine: *Memories*, Everleigh Nash & Grayson, 1924
Weintraub, Stanley (ed): *The Savoy – Nineties Experiment*, The Pennsylvania State University Press, 1966
Wintermans, Caspar: *Lord Alfred Douglas*, Peter Owen, 2007
Wright, Thomas: *Oscar's Books*, Chatto and Windus, 2008
Yeats, W.B.: *Mythologies*, Macmillan and Co, 1970
Yeats, W.B.: *Autobiographies*, Macmillan and Co, 1926

Articles & Ephemera
The Anti-Jacobean: 'The Cultured Faun' (as anon), 1891
The Chameleon: 'On the Appreciation of Trifles'. John Francis Bloxam (ed), 1894
The Outlook: 'A Great Unknown', 1899
The Catholic Society: 'By one who knew him' Obituary by Louise Imogen Guiney, 1902
The Daily Mail: 'A London Ghost: Inexplicable Happenings' & Obituary, 1901-2
The Criterion: Two letters to Louise Imogen Guiney, April 1925
'A Letter to Edgar Jepson': Iain Fletcher (ed) privately printed leaflet, 1979
Fortean Times: 'Winged Terror', Nina Antonia, May 2017
Wormwood: 'Lionel Johnson – The Disconsolate Decadent' Nina Antonia, Tartarus Press, Spring & Winter 2017

R. J. Holt · F.W. Rawlfoot · S. D. Bewley · A. W. Brewin · C.W. Little · R.T. Warren · S.F. Davidson · J.F.V. Russell · E.L. De Brett · P.N. Watkins ·
R. Wakefield · L.P. Johnson · H.L.D. Joseph · C. Dodgson · R.C. Fowler ·
J.C.G. Sykes · L.J. Palmer ·

Lionel Johnson *(middle row, second from left)* at Winchester College, 1884.

THREE ESSAYS

INCURABLE
from *The Pageant*, 1896.

Mist hung grey along the river, and upon the fields. From the cottage, little and lonely, shone candlelight, that looked sad to the wanderer without in the autumnal dark: he turned and faced the fields, and the dim river. And the music, the triumphing music, the rich voices of the violin, came sounding down the garden from the cottage. His mood, his mind, were those of the Flemish poet, who murmurs in sighing verse:

> *Et je suis dans la nuit... Oh! c'est si bon la nuit!*
> *Ne rien faire... se taire... et bercer son ennui,*
> *Au rhythm agonisant de lonitaine musique...*

For this was the last evening of his life: he felt sure of that: and, foolish martyr to his own weakness that he was, he fell to meditating upon the sad scenery and circumstances of his death. The grey mist upon river and field, the acrid odours of autumnal flowers in the garden, the solitariness of melancholy twilight, these were right and fitting: but there, in the cottage behind him, was his best friend, speaking with him through music, giving him his *Ave atque Vale* upon the violin. A choice incident! And instinctively he began to find phrases for it, plangent, mournful, suitable to the elegiac sonnet. True, his friend was not all that he could have wished: an excellent musician of common sense, well dressed and healthy, with nothing of Chopin about him, nothing of Paganini. But the sonnet need not mention the musician, only his music. So he looked at the dim river and the misty fields, and thought, of long, alliterative, melancholy words. Immemorial, irrevocable, visionary, marmoreal…

The Lyceum was responsible for this. That classic journal, reviewing his last book of verses, had told him that though he should vivisect his soul in public for evermore, he would find there nothing worth revealing, and nothing to compensate the spectators for their painful and pitying emotions. He had thought it a clumsy sarcasm, ponderous no less than rude: but he could not deny its truth. Tenderly opening his book, he lighted upon these lines:

> Ah, day by swift malignant day,
> Life vanishes in vanity:
> Whilst I, life's phantom victim, play
> The music of my misery.
> Draw near, ah dear delaying Death!
> Draw near, and silence my sad breath.

The lines touched him; yet he could not think them a valuable utterance: nor did he discover much fine gold in his sonnet, which began:

> Along each melancholy London street,
> Beneath the heartless stars, the indifferent moon,
> I walk with sorrow, and I know that soon
> Despair and I will walk with friendly feet.

It was good but Shakespeare and Keats, little as he could comprehend why, had done better. He had sat in his Temple chambers, nursing these dreary cogitations, for many hours of an October day, until the musician came to interrupt him: and to the violinist the versifier confessed.

'I am just thirty,' he began, 'and quite useless. I have a good education, and a little money. I must do something: and poetry is what I want to do. I have published three volumes, and they are entirely futile. They are not even bad enough to be interesting. I have not written one verse that anyone can remember. I have tried a great many styles, and I cannot write anything really good and fine in any one of them.' He turned over the leaves with a hasty and irritated hand. 'There, for instance! This is an attempt at the sensuous love-lyric: listen!

> Sometime, in very joy of shame,
> Our flesh becomes one living flame:
> And she and I
> Are no more separate but the same.
>
> Ardour and agony unite;
> Desire, delirium, delight:
> And I and she
> Faint in the fierce and fevered night.
>
> Her body music is: and ah,
> The accords of music and viola,
> When she and I
> Play on live limbs love's opera!

It's a lie, of course: but even if it were true, could anyone care to read it? Then why should I want to write it? And why can't I write better? I know what imagination is, and poetry, and all the rest of it. I go on contemplating my own emotions, or invent them and nothing comes of it but this. And yet I'm not a perfect fool.' 'That,' said the musician, 'is true, though it is not your fault: but you soon will be, if you go on maunderings like this by yourself. Come down to my cottage by the river, and invent a new profession.' And they went.

But the country is dangerous to persons of weak mind, who examine much the state of their emotions: they indulge there in delicious luxuries of introspection. The unhappy poet brooded upon his futility, with occasional desperate efforts to write something like the Ode to Duty or the Scholar Gypsy: dust and ashes! dust and ashes! Suddenly the horror of a long life spent in following the will-o'-the-wisp, or in questing for Sangrails and Eldorados, fell upon him: he refused to become an elderly mooncalf. The river haunted him with its facilities for death, and he regretted that there were no water-lilies on it: still, it was cold and swift and deep, overhung by alders, and edged by whispering reeds. Why not? He was of no use: if he went out to the colonies, or upon the stock exchange, he would continue to write quantities of average and uninteresting verse. It was his destiny: and the word pleased him. There was a certain distinction in having a destiny, and in defeating it by death. He had but a listless care for life, few ties that he would grieve to break, no prospects and ambitions within his reach. Upon this fourth evening then, he went down to the end of the garden and looked towards the river.

The sonnet was done at last, and he smiled to find himself admiring it. In all honesty, he fancied that death had inspired him well. He had read, surely he had read, worse sestets.

> I shall not hear what any morrow saith:
> I only hear this my last twilight say
> Cease thee from signing and from bitter breath,

For all thy life with autumn mist is grey!
Dirged by loud music, down to silent death
I pass, and on the waters pass away.

A pity that it should be lost: but to leave it upon the bank would be almost an affectation. Besides, there was pathos in dying with his best verses upon his lips: verses that only he and the twilight should hear. Night fell fast and very gloomy, with scarce a star. Leaning upon the gate, he tried to remember the names of modern poets who had killed themselves: Chatterton, Gerard de Nerval. They, at least, could write poetry, and their failure was not in art. Yet he could live his poetry, as Milton and Carlyle, he thought, had recommended: live it by dying, because he could not write it. 'What Cato did and Addison approved' had its poetical side: and no one without a passion for poetry would die in despair at failure in it. The violin sent dancing into the night an exhilarating courtly measure of Rameau: 'The Dance of Death!' said the poet, and was promptly ashamed of so obvious and hackneyed a sentiment. At the same time, there was something strange and rare in drowning yourself by night to the dance-music of your unconscious friend.

The bitter smell of aster and chrysanthemum was heavy on the air; 'balms and rich spices for the sad year's death,' as he had once written: and he fancied, though he could not be sure, that he caught a bat's thin cry. The 'pathetic fallacy' was extremely strong upon him, and he pitied himself greatly. To die so futile and so young! A minor Hamlet with Ophelia's death! And at this his mind turned to Shakespeare, and to a famous modern picture, and to the Lady of Shalott. He imagined himself floating down and down to some mystical medieval city, its torchlights flashing across his white face. But for that, he should be dressed differently; in something Florentine perhaps: certainly not in a comfortable smoking-coat by a London tailor. And at that, he was reminded that a last cigarette would not be out of place: he lighted one, and presently fell to wondering whether he was mad or no. He thought not: he was sane enough to know that he would never write great poetry, and to die sooner than waste life in the misery of vain efforts. The last wreath of smoke gone upon the night, not without a comparison between the wreath and himself, he opened the garden gate, and walked gently down the little field, at the end of which ran the river. He went through the long grass, heavy with dew, looking up at the starless sky, and into the impenetrable darkness. Of a sudden, with the most vivid surprise of his life, he fell forward, with a flashing sensation of icy water bubbling round his face, blinding and choking him; of being swirled and carried along; of river weeds clinging round his head; of living in a series of glimpses and visions. Mechanically striking out across stream, he reached the bank, steadied and rested himself for an instant by the branch of an overhanging alder, then climbed ashore. There he lay and shivered; then, despite the cold, tingled with shame, and blushed; then laughed; lastly, got up and shouted. The shout rose discordantly above the musician's harmonies, and he heard someone call his name. 'It's just that moon-struck poet of mine,' said he, and went down to the gate. 'Is that you?' he cried, 'and where are you?' And out of the darkness beyond came the confused and feeble answer – 'I fell into the river – and I'm on the wrong side.' The practical man wasted no words, but made for the boathouse, where he kept his punt: and in a few minutes the shivering poet dimly descried his rescuer in mid-stream. The lumbering craft grounded and the drowned man, with stiff and awkward movement got himself on board. 'What do you mean,' said the musician, 'by making me play Charon on this ghostly river at such an hour?' 'I was-thinking of things,' said the poet, 'and it was pitch dark – and I fell in.' They landed; and the dewy field, the autumnal garden, the rich night air, seemed to be mocking him. His teeth chattered, and he shook, and still he mumbled bits of verse. Said the musician as they entered the little cottage: 'The first thing for you to do is to take off those things, and have hot drinks in bed, like Mr. Pickwick.' Said the doomed man, quaking like an aspen: 'Yes, but I must write out a sonnet first, before I forget it.' He did.

THE CULTURED FAUN
Published anonymously in *The Anti-Jacobin*, 1891.

He, or shall we say it? Is a curious creature; tedious after a time, when you have got its habits by heart, but certainly curious on first acquaintance. You breed it in this way:

Take a young man, who had brains as a boy, and teach him to disbelieve everything his elders believe in matters of thought and to reject everything that seems true to himself in matters of sentiment. He need not be at all revolutionary; most clever youths for mere experience's sake will discard their natural or acquired convictions. He will then, since he is intelligent and bright, want something to replace his early notions. If Aristotle's *Poetics* are absurd, and Pope is no poet, and politics are vulgar, and Carlyle is played out, and Mr. Ruskin is tiresome, and so forth, according to the circumstances of the case, our youth will be bored to death by the nothingness of everything. You must supply him with the choicest delicacies, and feed him upon the finest rarities. And what so choice as a graceful affectation, or so fine as a surprising paradox? So you cast about for these two, and at once you see that many excellent affectations and paradoxes have had their day. A treasured melancholy of the German moonlight sort, a rapt enthusiasm in the Byronic style, a romantic eccentricity after the French fashion of 1830, a "frank, fierce, sensuousness *a la jeunesse Swinburnienne*", our youth might flourish them in the face of society all at once, without receiving a single invitation to private views or suppers of the elect. And, in truth, it requires a positive genius for the absurd to discover a really promising affectation, a thoroughly fascinating paradox. But the last ten years have done it. And a remarkable achievement it is.

Externally, our hero should cultivate a reassuring sobriety of habit, with just a dash of the dandy. None of the wandering looks, the elaborate disorder, the sublime lunacy of his predecessor, the "apostle of culture." Externally, then, a precise appearance, internally, a catholic sympathy with all that exists, and "therefore" suffers, for art's sake. Now art, at present, is not a question of the senses so much as of the nerves. Botticelli, indeed was very precious but Baudelaire is very nervous. Gautier was adorably sensuous, but M. Verlaine is pathetically sensitive. That is the point: exquisite appreciation of pain, exquisite thrills of anguish, exquisite adoration of suffering. Here comes in a tender patronage of Catholicism: white tapers upon the high altar, an ascetic and beautiful young priest, the great gilt monstrance, the subtle scented and mystical incense, the old world accents of the Vulgate, of the Holy Offices; the splendour of the sacred vestments. We kneel at some hour, not too early for our convenience, repeating that solemn Latin, drinking in those Gregorian tones, with plenty of modern French sonnets in memory, should the sermon be dull. But to join the Church! Ah, no! better to dally with the enchanting mysteries, to pass from our dreams of delirium to our dreams of sanctity with no coarse facts to jar upon us. And so these refined persons cherish a double "passion," the sentiment of repentant yearning and the sentiment of rebellious sin.

To play the part properly a flavour of cynicism is recommended: a scientific profession of materialist dogmas, coupled – for you should forswear consistency – with gloomy chatter about "The Will to Live." If you can say it in German, so much the better: a gross tongue, partially redeemed by Heine, but an infallible oracle of scepticism. Jumble all these "impressions!" together, your sympathies and your sorrows, your devotion and your despair; carry them about with you in a state of fermentation, and finally conclude that life is loathsome yet beauty is beatific. And beauty – ah, beauty is everything beautiful! Isn't that a trifle obvious, you say? That is the charm of it, it shows your perfect simplicity, your chaste and catholic innocence. Innocence of course: beauty is always innocent, ultimately. No doubt there are "monstrous" things, terrible pains, the haggard eyes of an *absinteur*, the pallid faces of "neurotic" sinners; but all that is the portion of our Parisian friends, such and such a "group of artists," who meet at the Café So-and-So. We like people to think we are much the same, but it isn't true. We are quite harmless, we only concoct strange and subtle verse about it. And, anyway, beauty includes everything; there's another sweet saying for you from our "impressionist" copy-books. Impressions! That is all. Life is mean and vulgar, Members of Parliament are odious, the critics are commercial pedants: we alone know Beauty, and Art, and Sorrow, and Sin. Impressions! exquisite, dainty fantasies; fiery-coloured visions; and impertinence straggling into epigram, for "the true" criticism; *c'est adorable*! And since we are scholars and none of your penny-a-line Bohemians, we throw in occasional doses of "Hellenism": by which we mean the Ideal of the Cultured Faun. That is to say a flowery Paganism, such as no "Pagan" ever had; a mixture of "beautiful woodland natures," and "the perfect comeliness of the Parthenon frieze," together with the elegant languors and favourite vices of (let us parade our "decadent" learning) the *Stratonis Epigrammata** this time of day we need not dilate upon the equivocal charm of everything Lesbian. And who shall assail us? – what stupid uncultured critic, what coarse and narrow Philistines? We are the Elect of Beauty: saints and sinners, devils and devotees, Athenians and Parisians, Romans of the Empire and Italians of the Renaissance. *Fin de siècle! Fin de siècle!* Literature is a thing of beauty, blood and nerves.

Let the Philistine critic have the last word; let him choose his words with all care, and define in his rough fashion. How would it do to call the Cultured Faun a feeble and a foolish beast?

*Epigrams of Straton, which appeared in the Greek Anthology, most of which are dedicated to homosexuality.

ON THE APPRECIATION OF TRIFLES
From *The Chameleon*, 1894.

It is a sad saying, and one that, although frequently quoted, is nevertheless true: the Art of Living has almost become one of the lost arts.

In order to understand the art of living, and in order to become oneself an artist, it is necessary to discover the true secret of life. The true secret of life, as has been well pointed out, is this: to understand that there is in truth no secret at all. That is why we waste the beauty of our youth and cast away from us in our ignorant folly the splendid chances with which our young life is beset. There is no secret; and therefore men frequently spend their whole life searching for one. If we would but look around us we should see that the whole mystery of life is ours, ours to grasp and toy with, ours to taste of and enjoy. To each of us life comes and whispers, 'See, there are beautiful delights set close beside you; to appreciate the delights that are at hand is to taste life in all its sweet completeness. Why must you waste yourself in searching for the vague, imaginary phantoms of a secret that does not exist? Oh, why can you not open your eyes and see? But we are as those that stop their ears; we pay no heed to these soft whisperings. If we hear them at all – for there are those that fail even to do that – we shrink aside and murmur 'that we must overcome temptation.' We miss the beauty of life in the foolishness of our poor, short-sighted minds, and then boast that we possess a 'conscience'!

The true secret of life is not set beyond our reach on the snow-laden summits of the difficult mountains, struggling to surmount whose precipices so many waste their youth; it need not be sought beneath the torrent of the swift running waters of adversity: the true secret is ready at our hand each day we live. It is not to be found with the toil of learning; it is the mystery that is revealed to babes.

The terrible mistake that mars the beauty of so many lives lies in the idea of only seeking enjoyment in great things: as is often said, the real pleasure of life consists in the little details, the scarce-considered trifles of every day. It is in these little superfluous pleasures that we can – if only we have eyes to see – find balm for the soul that is troubled and incense to soothe the nerves that are overwrought. It is grievous to see these various little trifles of life slurred over and neglected: they afford such unbounded opportunities for the development and cultivation of the senses.

Perhaps there is nothing that tends so surely towards the deadening of the senses as the practice of economy. Economy is a grievous evil, but it would be foolish to deny that to many of us it is an evil that is unavoidable. It is one of those stern realities of life that must be faced, use what paradox and epigram we may. But it is in the practice of the vicious habit that we are apt to stray so far from the delicate path of the beautiful. We are so foolish, we persist in denying ourselves the little, inexpensive luxuries that touch us most closely every day; it is by denying ourselves these in order to save a few pence that we lose the art of living. Let us be very prosaic for a moment and take perhaps the most homely example possible – homely, but full of sweet possibilities – soap! For the additional expenditure of some small fraction of a penny each day we can indulge our senses continually by the use of soap the most delicious and costly! Again, I have often heard use of perfume denounced as extravagant. The expenditure of five shillings on such a mere luxury as this is most stringently forbidden by these devotees of false economy. For this small sum perfume of the most exquisite fragrance can be purchased, and the cost when compared with the consequent enjoyment cannot fail to sink into complete insignificance. The use of it does not merely affect one for the second occupied in sprinkling a few drops over the hands, handkerchief and hair: it is a lasting delight that tints the whole day with a faint, indescribable hue; it gladdens the senses; by some mysterious process of delicate refinement it seems to screen us from the cares and trials of the day with a fragrant, rose-tinged veil of unreality. The false economist saves his five shillings, it is true; but he knows not this rare solace, this dream-laden narcotic for mental anxiety.

The unfortunate man who is really in the clutches of this demoralising vice seems almost proud of his degradation; he embraces his fetters, and delights in any opportunity of demonstrating how closely they confine him. Especially he rejoices his heart by seriously incommoding his body to effect some quite infinitesimal saving. I have frequently, when travelling seen a lighted lucifer handed completely round a railway-carriage, to avoid more than one being 'wasted.' I have marked with a pitying smile the eagerness in the eyes of the occupant of a distant corner as he watches anxiously to see if the match will survive until it reaches him. I have marked the expression of pain on the face of each slave to economy as he takes the precious object of all this care and interest in his hand, invariably suffering untold agonies, both mental and physical, in the process. I have also experienced this delight, I say, as I have politely refused the proffered lucifer, passing my own match-box instead.

Let us not, however, confine ourselves entirely to the distressing side of this most important question. There are many whose lives are a constant protest against this vice and the evil practice it entails. I, personally, have the pleasure of possessing quite a large number of very charming friends who are entirely lacking in economy in any form whatsoever.

But it is in other ways than economy that we stint our senses and waste our opportunities of self-indulgence. We have no idea of making the beautiful our aim in trifles. We make a point, as far as the supremacy of bad taste will allow us, of decorating our public buildings and beautifying our parks. Lately many of us have even made an effort to introduce graceful line and melodious colouring into our drawing rooms. But the great mistake still remains; those little details with which we are most continually coming into contact remain untouched in all their ugliness. For instance, what is more ugly and what is in more constant use than a railway ticket? Some attempt has lately been made abroad to alter the nature of this, to so many, daily necessity. A bow of ribbon has been adopted, the colour varying in accordance with the class. Unfortunately, this idea, because it aims at convenience and utility instead of the beautiful, is an obvious failure. It is rather vulgar, and is likely to give rise to certain complications. In the first place, because certain people of our acquaintance would enter a first-class carriage with considerably less composure than they assume today; in the second place, because it would be distinctly annoying, when some unexpected cause may call us to choose a particular compartment, to thus announce to any unconcerned occupants of the carriage that our proper class was first and not third.

No: beyond all doubt, nothing of the nature of a badge must receive our support.

Again, what a splendid opportunity of beautifying a necessary is thrown away at the majority of our theatres. A few – all praise to them – have adopted programmes that possess real elements of artistic beauty; but a far larger number presents us with a vulgar example of the bad taste of the cheap printer and the blatant insufficiency of the successful advertiser.

If we wish for still further proof of our failure to apply to the concerns of the day, let us stroll round the exhibition of posters at the Aquarium. How astonished and amazed, perhaps even shocked, should we be if one morning we were to find our hoardings flaring with the audacious beauty of these French posters! Did we not in very fact hold up our hands in half-fearful surprise at the first appearance of some of the darling artistic ventures of Mr. Dudley Hardy? And do not the Philistines rage furiously together each time Mr. Aubrey Beardsley imagines a vain thing? This is a curious point to note – our lack of appreciation when these details are rendered beautiful.

But in spite of the fact that the influence of the middle classes tends towards the degradation of our sense of the beautiful, we can find almost unlimited sources of artistic pleasure if we will but look around us. Curiously enough, many of these details that are most pleasing to the aesthetic sense were not designed with the smallest view to beauty.

Of course, compared with the arrangement of the shop windows in Paris, our own must appear painfully crude; nevertheless, it is always a comfort to feel that at any moment, by a turn of the head, we can behold a full-length reflection of our own persons almost as perfectly as a mirror. But, setting aside this constant source of aesthetic gratification, there is much of beauty to be noticed in our streets at any time. Although I pride myself on appreciating to the full the charming picturesqueness of rags, I cannot help feeling that the appearance of our streets owes very much to the present system of dressing all officials and private servants in more or less becoming uniforms and liveries. I am sure we must all constantly feel that we are under the deepest obligations to certain companies and, strangely enough, to the Government officials connected with the Post Office, for filling our streets with the graceful, neatly uniformed figures of those that bear our messages and our telegrams.

It is said that the characteristics of a nation are revealed more clearly in the matter of eating and drinking than in any other way. The English middle classes subsist almost entirely on what is, I believe, most descriptively called 'butcher's meat.' This diet, I am afraid, shows a most lamentable lack of the appreciation of trifles.

Perhaps it is better so; if the average Philistine were to be civilised and were suddenly to become enamoured of the beauty of those trifles that today are the exclusive enjoyment of the artists, we should feel the loss of his quaint antics very keenly. It would be very sad if we were to lose that great delight to which I alluded earlier: it would be very sad if there were no one left to shock.

OFFICERS 1885

Johnson Wakefield JOSEPH Fowler Dodgson

Lionel Johnson *(left)* at Winchester College, 1885.

POEMS

A Dream

Did I ever tell you a strange kind of dream I had a few months ago? I was sleeping quietly when I felt a shock go right through me, and I seemed to have left my body behind, and gone off to the stars; I saw myriads of lights streaming over and on a vast white lake: I was in a state of perfect ecstasy, when I felt myself whirled back to my body, and woke up with a violent sense of splitting headache. I at once got up while the impression was fresh and vivid, and wrote down an exact record of my impressions in a poem: It is now somewhat unintelligible, but absolutely accurate as a faithful record of immense sensations and influences. I have never experienced anything like it before or since.

One night far up amongst the white stars dreaming
    I knew my soul wafted away from me,
To where a clear coruscant light was gleaming
    And shot forth rays across a stilly sea.

The air was laden with chilling numbness
    And then my soul felt sudden iron hands
Strike through her utterance a thrill of dumbness
    And gird her round with thwarting steely bands.

She moved not, neither knew the fateful region
    Only the glare of white eye-dazzling rays,
Only the blue, dark sea and many a legion
    Of fluttering stars and spirits of unknown days.

These only marked she and with timid wonder
    Gazed upon hosts of alternating light;
And ever and anon the scene asunder
    Was cleft by radiance of higher might.

Faint with much straining of her eyes, she inward
    Turned them, and in her secret self she mused,
Whether she now were feebly staring sinward
    And her true seeing ruthlessly abused.

Or if to glories of the highest heaven
    These fitful blinding darts guided the way;
And iron bands for strengthening staves were given
    And she were gazing in the sunward day.

While thus she mused, she felt a stirring motion
    Of tossing surges, and of restless seas;
And turning toward the sound, the purple ocean
    She saw besprinkled with pale phantasies.

And to her eyes their form was as of strangers
    That know not where to turn nor how to rest,
And hover listlessly o'er quaking dangers
    And fain would sleep upon a serpent's breast.

Then as she downward gazed upon them lying,
    Around her flowed a sea of shimmering light
And countless images she saw, all flying
    Down to the waves with headlong wings of flight.

And as they touched the waters, straight a terror
    Of frantic billows rose, and clashing tides,
And currents seethed in multitudinous error,
    And all was noise, where nought of rest abides.

No more she knew, but when her aching senses
    Once more were quickened then in wondering wise
She felt herself a part of piercing lenses
    Through which all things were seen by fearful eyes.

A weird expansion felt she of her nature,
    Whereby she shared in all the world around
And she became a part of every creature
    And was transfused in every sight and sound.

Yet still she hung aloft in starry places
    And felt the floods of light upon her life;
But of the sea were gone all heaving traces,
    And only light clove light in dazzling strife

White stars marched on and on in high procession,
    And aeons came with steps of stately feet;
And in the heavenly arc was no transgression,
    And moons still rose and sank, still silver sweet.

Only a quickening current stirred the spirit
     Of life, and self died from the range of things,
A brother's love was each man's to inherit,
     And soul met soul with other seeking wings.

The vision fled before my eyelids waking
     And to the glare succeeded blinding night
As back to earth her way my soul was taking
     And the sun rose upon the face of night.

I care not greatly for the stress of anguish
     But ah! that I might pierce the veil that shrouds
The unseen world, that I no more might languish
     With eyes that ache to cleave the heavy clouds.

Thus once I cried but now I cry no longer,
     To send my soul to realms of eterne light,
Heaven's rays than my poor soul are ever stronger,
     And heavenly stars too strong for my poor sight.

July, 1883

I am indebted to Iain Fletcher's textural notes in *The Complete Poems of Lionel Johnson* (Unicorn Press, 1953). As editor, Fletcher thought to include an explanatory extract from *The Winchester Letters* written by Lionel in November, 1883, as a preface to the visionary poem 'A Dream', which I too have included. (NA)

Light! For the Stars Are Pale

"Non, Pavenir n'est a personne" *Hugo*
"Les morts, les pauvres morts, ont de grandes douleurs."
Baudelaire

Light! For the stars are pale; light! For the high moon
        wanes;
Whither now hides the sun, that all we stricken blind,
Feel not his eyes, hear not the thunders of the wind
Flung round him trumpet-toned about his clear domain?
Morn's rose along night's verge with folded wing disdains
Our twilight miserable and hopes of humankind,
Hardly we catch its breath: is the great sun less kind,
Than falling stars, frail moons, than night's cloud
        hurricanes?

Darkling we dwindle deathward, and our dying sight
Strains back to pierce the living gloom; ere night be done
We pass from night to night; our sons shall see the light,
Children of us shall laugh to welcome the free sun;
Yet pity for the poor dead must mar their fair joy won;
That all we died too soon, passing from night to night.

from *The Wykehamist*
26 June, 1885

Evening In Wales
To Hubert Cornish

Laughing at our cold despair,
Spring is come: laud we her name!
Out into this gentler air,
Musical with breath that came
Over seas and islands, where
Suns have fragrance in their flame:
Come with me, and let soft wind
Soothe the chambers of your mind.

Starrier anemones,
Than rich southern woods enfold;
Heavenlier coloured primroses,
Than fair southern maids behold;
Hushed by Alun's cadences,
Kinglier marsh marigold:
Seeing these, be proud to praise
Wales with all her flowered ways.

With no grace of Cyclad peaks,
Gleaming crowns for seas of light;
Moel Fammau darkling seeks
Converse with the coming night:
Purple shadowed, how she breaks
The red splendours, out of sight
Fading, until dewy morn
Bid them with new fire be born!

1886

Hubert Warre Cornish was the son of the Vice-Principal of
Eton. His association with Lionel is unknown.

Upon Reading Certain Poems

I come, a lost wind from the shores
Of wondering dull misery:
With muttered echoes, heartsick plaints,
And sullen sorrows, filling me.
But all this flowery world abhors
Me, wretched wind and heavy cloud:
Beneath me, as beneath a shroud,
    The spirit of summer faints.

The golden angel of delight
Gleams past me, and I shrink away:
A dimness on the dawn am I,
A mist upon a merry day.
Here should be none but Muses bright,
Whose airs go delicately sweet:
With swallow wings, and faery feet,
    Eager to dance or fly.

I will drift back to Wearyland,
To wondering dull misery:
No champaign rich, nor rosy lawn,
Shall wither by the fault of me.
Where no one takes loved hand in hand,
But with his shadow crawls alone:
They miss the comfort of my moan,
    My melancholy long-drawn.

1887

Bells
To John Little

From far away! from far away!
    But whence you will not say:
Melancholy bells, appealing chimes,
    Voices of lands and times!

Your toll, O melancholy bells!
    Over the valley swells:
O touching chimes! your dying sighs
    Travel our tranquil skies.

But whence! And whither fade away
    Your echoes from our day?
You take our hearts with gentle pain,
    Tremble, and pass again.

Could we lay hold upon your haunts,
    The birthplace of your chaunts:
Were we in dreamland, deathland, then?
    We, sad and wondering men?

1887

John David George Little was an Oxford contemporary of the poet.

Incense
To Miss Alice Brown

1

All the annulling clouds, that lie
Far in wait for years to come,
Shall not force me to forget
All the witcheries of home,
While in the world there linger yet
Heliotrope and mignonette:
In their scent home cannot die.

When the delicate dewdrops gleamed
Tremulous on the early blooms;
The full sweetness of the dawn,
Gathered during twilight glooms,
Rose above the fields and lawn,
Ravishing me with fragrance drawn
From each flower, that there had dreamed.

Then was innocent glory shed
All about the garden ground:
Gods of Helicon well had paced
By the laurels, and around
The bright lawn; nor deemed disgraced
Their high Godhead, nor misplaced
Their descent, since thither led

By a maze of gossamer dew
Measured by the pasture leas:
Ruddy gray the sunlight glanced
Through the rippling poplar trees,
On the airy webs, where chanced
Dainty faery feet had danced
Without noise, the soft night through.

That was morn indeed! And yet,
Gone the wondrous witchery;
Gone the charm, the enchauntment gone;
Still to aging memory
Come the scents, the lights that shone,
That were sweet: dreams lie upon
Heliotrope and mignonette.

Stronger than remembered looks,
Nearer than old written words,
Cling the loved old fragrances;
At the matin time of birds,
Giving birth to memories:
Not one fancy perishes,
Born before we woke to books.

All will come again: once more
We shall fling our arms upon
Morning's wind and ravish yet
All its load of incense, won
From rich wilding mignonette,
Clustered heliotrope, and wet
Meadows, O fair years of yore!

11

They do the will of beauty and regret,
Odours and travelling faery fragrances:
The breath of things, I never can forget,
The haunting spirit of old memories.
Gray grows the visible world; fair cadences
Break into death: sweet are the field flowers yet.

Softly at evening, hard upon twilight,
Old earth breathes balmy air on hushing winds,
And takes with ravishment the face of night.
Pensive and solitary old age finds
Calm in the vesperal, mild air, that minds
His dwindling hour, of childhood's far delight.

A breath, a thought, a dream! Ah, what a choir
Of long stilled voices: and of long closed eyes,
What a light! So came, so mine heart's desire
Came through the pinewood, where the sunlight dies
Tonight. Since now these fragrant memories
Live, lives not also she, their soul of fire?

1887

American novelist, Alice Brown was a friend of Louise Imogen Guiney, and was later her biographer.

Summer Storm
To Harold Child

The wind, hark! The wind in the angry woods:
And how clouds purple the west: there broods
    Thunder, thunder; and rain will fall;
Fresh fragrance cling to the wind from all
    Roses holding water wells,
Laurels gleaming to the gusty air;
    Wilding mosses of the dells,
Drenched hayfields, and ripping hedgerows fair.

The wind, hark! the wind dying again:
The wind's voice matches the far-off main,
    In sighing cadences: Pan will wake,
Pan in the forest, whose rich pipes make
    Music to the folding flowers,
In the pure eve, where no hot spells are:
    Those be favourable hours
Hymned by Pan beneath the shepherd star.

1887

Author & journalist, Harold Hannyngton Child (1869-1945) attended Winchester & Oxford, with Lionel.

Magic
To John Myres

1

Because I work not, as logicians work
Who but ranked and marshalled reason yield:
But my feet hasten through a faery field,
Thither, where underneath the rainbow lurk
Spirits of youth, and life, and gold concealed:

Because by leaps I scale the secret sky,
Upon the motion of a cunning star:
Because I hold the winds oracular,
And think on airy warnings, when men die:
Because I tread the ground, where shadows are:

Therefore my name is grown a popular scorn,
And I a children's terror! Only now,
For I am old! O Mother Nature! Thou
Leavest me not: wherefore, as night turns morn,
A magician wisdom breaks beneath my brow.

These painful toilers of the bounded way,
Chaired within cloister halls: can they renew
Ashes to flame? Can they of moonlit dew
Prepare the immortalizing draughts? Can they
Give gold for refuse earth, or bring to view

Earth's deepest doings? Let them have their school,
Their science, and their safety! I am he,
Whom Nature fills with her philosophy,
And takes for kinsmen. Let me be their fool,
And wise man in the wind's society.

1887

11

They wrong with ignorance a royal choice,
Who cavil at my loneliness and labour:
For them the luring wonder of a voice,
The viol's cry for them, the harp and tabour:
    For me divine austerity,
    And voices of philosophy.

Ah! light imagination, that discern
No passion in the citadel of passion:
Their fancies lie on flowers; but my thoughts turn
To thoughts and things of an eternal fashion:
    The majesty and dignity
    Of everlasting verity.

Mine is the sultry sunset, when the skies
Tremble with strange, intolerable thunder:
And at the dead of an hushed night, these eyes
Draw down the soaring oracles winged with wonder:
    From the four winds they come to me,
    The Angels of Eternity.

Men pity me; poor men, who pity me!
Poor, charitable, scornful souls of pity!
I choose laborious loneliness: and ye
Lead Love in triumph through the dancing city:
    While death and darkness girdle me,
     I grope for immortality.

1887

111

Pour slowly out your holy balm of oil,
Within the grassy circle: let none spoil
Our favourable silence. Only I,
Winding wet vervain round mine eyes, will cry
Upon the powerful Lord of this our toil;
Until the first lark sing, the last star die.

Proud Lord of twilight, Lord of Midnight, hear!
Thou hast forgone us; and has drowsed thine ear,
When haggard voices hail thee: thou hast turned
Blind eyes, dull nostrils, when our vows have burned
Herbs on the moonlit flame, in reverent fear:
Silence is all, our love of thee hath earned.

Master! we call thee, calling on thy name!
Thy savoury laurel crackles: the blue flame
Gleams, leaps, devours apace the dewy leaves
Vain! For nor breast of labouring midnight heaves,
Nor chilled stars fall: all things remain the same,
Save this new pang, that stings, and burns and cleaves.

Despising us, thou knowest not! We stand.
Bared for thine adoration, hand in hand:
Steely our eyes, our hearts to all but thee
Iron: as waves of the unresting sea,
The wind of thy least Word is our command:
And our ambition hails thy sovereignty.

Come, sisters! For the King of night is dead:
Come! For the frailest star of stars hast sped:
And though we waited for the waiting sun,
Our King would wake not. Come! Our world is done:
For all the witchery of the world is fled,
And lost all wanton wisdom long since won.

1888

Myres, a contemporary of Lionel's at Winchester & New College,
subsequently taught ancient history at Oxford.

The End
To Austin Ferrand

I gave you more than love: many times more:
I gave you mine honour into your fair keeping.
You lost mine honour: wherefore now restore
The love, I gave, not dead, but cold and sleeping
You loveless, I dishonoured, go our ways:
Dead is the past, dead must be all my days.

Death and the shadows tarry not: fulfil
Your years with folly and love's imitation
You had mine all: mine only now, to kill
All trembling memories of mine adoration.
That done, to lie me down, and die, and dream,
What once, I thought you were: what still you seem.

1887

Austin & his brother, Alfred, were friends of Lionel's. After a
brief foray into literary life, the brothers relocated to South Africa.
Alfred, who joined the Imperial Light Horse Regiment, perished
at Ladysmith on January 6th, 1900, whilst Austin fell to a Boer
bullet, six months later. Their deaths seem to have taken a heavy
toll on Johnson.

Old Silver

Behold, what thrones of the Most High
Are here within the common mart!
    True God hath entered
    These crystal-centred,
Silvern stars: Men! Come and buy,
    If you have the heart!

Melt down the royal throne, break up
The sanctuary of Deity!
    Is then God's glory
    So transitory,
Mortal men? Christ! Is Thy Cup
    But a memory?

1887

Dead
To Olivier Georges Destree

In Merioneth, over the sad moor
    Drives the rain, the cold wind blows:
    Past the ruinous church door,
The poor procession without music goes.

Lonely she wandered out her hour, and died.
    Now the mournful curlew cries
    Over her, laid down beside
Death's lonely people: lightly down she lies.

In Merioneth, the wind lives and wails,
    On from hill to lonely hill:
    Down the loud, triumphant gales,
A spirit cries *Be strong!* and cries *Be still!*

1887

Belgian poet, Olivier Georges Destree (1865-1919) subsequently joined a Benedictine Order.

Celtic Speech
To Dr Douglas Hyde

Never forgetful silence fall on thee,
    Nor younger voices overtake thee,
Nor echoes from thine ancient hills forsake thee;
Old music heard by Mona of the sea:
And where with moving melodies there break thee
Pastoral Conway, venerable Dee.

Like music lives, nor may that music die,
    Still in the far, fair Gaelic places:
The speech, so wistful with its kindly graces,
Holy Croagh Patricks knows, and Holy Hy:
The speech, that wakes the soul in withered faces,
And wakes remembrance of great things gone by.

Like music by the desolate Land's End
    Mournful forgetfulness hath broken:
No more words kindred to the winds are spoken,
Where upon iron cliffs who seas expend
That strength, whereof the unalterable token
Remains wild music, even to the world's end.

1887

The first President of the Irish Republic, Dr Douglas Hyde (1860-1949) also wrote *The Love Songs of Connaught* & *Songs Ascribed to Raferty*.

Late Love

When I had thought to make an home with sorrow,
    A gentle, melancholy dwelling;
    And there to linger life with telling
Over old fancies of some fair tomorrow:
    Sudden, there broke about my way
    Laughter, and flowers, and break of day.

Sing, Guardian Angel! One is come, who takes me
    Home to the land of loving voices:
    And there my loving heart rejoices
To tell each sorrow over, that forsakes me;
    And all the unimagined songs,
    That a child's carolling voice prolongs.

1887

Nihilism
To Samuel Smith

Among immortal things not made with hands;
Among immortal things, dead hands have made:
Under the Heavens, upon the Earth, there stands
Man's life, my life: of life I am afraid.

Where silent things, and unimpassioned things,
Where things of nought, and things decaying are:
I shall be calm soon, with the calm, death brings.
The skies are gray there, without any star.

Only the rest! the rest! Only the gloom,
Soft and long gloom! The pausing from all thought!
My life, I cannot taste: the eternal tomb
Brings me the peace, which life has never brought

For all the things I do, and do not well;
All the forced drawings of mortal breath:
Are as the hollow music of a bell,
That times the slow approach of perfect death.

1888

Samuel Smith (1867-1938) was a good friend of Ernest Dowson, with whom he corresponded for many years. After studying at Queen's College, Smith became a teacher and was also known for his translation of *Lysistrata*.

Mystic and Cavalier
To Herbert Percy Horne

Go from me: I am one of those, who fall.
What! Hath no cold wind swept your heart at all,
In my sad company? Before the end,
      Go from me, dear my friend!

Yours are the victories of light: your feet
Rest from good toil, where rest is brave and sweet.
But after warfare in a mourning gloom,
      I rest in clouds of doom.

Have you not read so, looking in these eyes?
Is it the common light of the pure skies,
Lights up their shadowy depths? The end is set:
      Though the end be not yet.

When gracious music stirs, and all is bright,
And beauty triumphs through a courtly night;
When I too joy, a man like other men:
      Yet, am I like them, then?

And in the battle, when the horsemen sweep
Against a thousand deaths, and fall on sleep:
Who ever sought that sudden calm, if I
      Sought not? Yet, could not die.

Seek with thine eyes to pierce this crystal sphere:
Canst read a fate there, prosperous and clear?
Only the mists, only the weeping clouds:
    Dimness and airy shrouds.

Beneath, what angels are at work? What powers
Prepare the secret of the fatal hours?
See! The mists tremble, and the clouds are stirred:
    When comes the calling word?

The clouds are breaking from the crystal ball,
Breaking and clearing: and I look to fall.
When the cold winds and airs of portent sweep,
    My spirit may have sleep.

O rich and sound voices of the air!
Interpreters and prophets of despair:
Priests of a fearful sacrament! I come,
    To make with you mine home.

1889

An architect as well as a historian of art and poetry, Herbert Percy Horne (1865-1916) was a mainstay of *The Century Guild Hobby Horse*. Horne designed Johnson's 1895 edition of *Poems*, which was published by Elkin Matthews.

Winchester

To the fairest!
                    Then to thee
Consecrate and bounden be,
Winchester! This verse of mine.
Ah, that loveliness of thine!
To have lived enchaunted years
Free from sorrows, free from fears,
Where thy Tower's great shadow falls
Over these proud buttressed walls;
Whence a purpling glory pours
From high heaven's inheritors,
Throned within the arching stone!
To have wandered, hushed, alone,
Gently round thy fair, fern-grown
Chauntry of the Lilies, lying
Where the soft night winds go sighing
Round thy Cloisters, in moonlight
Branching dark, or touched with white:
Round old, chill aisles, where moon-smitten
Blanches the *Orate*, written
Under each worn, old-world face
Graven on Death's holy place!

To the noblest!
                    None but thee
Blest our living eyes, that see
Half a thousand years fulfilled
Of that age, which Wykeham willed

Thee to win; yet all unworn,
As upon that first March morn,
When thine honoured city saw
The young beauty without flaw,
Born within her water-flowing,
Ancient hollows, by wind-blowing
Hills enfolded ever more.
Thee, that lord of splendid lore,
Orient from old Hellas' shore,
Grocyn, had to mother: thee,
Monumental majesty
Of most high philosophy
Honours, in thy wizard Browne:
Tender Otways's dear renown,
Mover of a perfect pity,
Victim of the iron city,
Thine to cherish is, and thee,
Laureate of Liberty;
Harper of the Highland faith,
Elf, and faery and wan wraith;
Chaunting softly, chaunting slowly,
Minstrel of all melancholy;
Master of all melody,
Made to cling round memory;
Passion's poet, Evening's voice,
Collins glorified. Rejoice,
Mother! In thy sons: for all
Love thine immemorial
Name, august and musical.
Not least he, who left thy side,

For his sire's, thine earlier pride,
Arnold: whom we mourn to-day,
Prince of song, and gone away
To his brothers of the bay:
Thine the love of all his years;
His be now thy praising tears.

To the dearest!
                                        Ah, to thee!
Hast thou not in all to me
Mother, more than mother, been?
Well toward thee may Mary Queen
Bend her with a mother's mien;
Who so rarely dost express
An inspiring tenderness,
Woven with thy sterner strain,
Prelude of the world's true pain.
But two years, and still my feet
Found the very stones more sweet,
Than the richest fields elsewhere:
Two years, and thy sacred air
Still poured balm upon me, when
Nearer drew the world of men;
When the passions, one by one,
All sprang upward to the sun:
Two years have I lived, still thine;
Lost, thy presence! gone, that shrine,
Where six years, what years! Were mine.
Music is the thought of thee;
Fragrance, all thy memory.

Those thy rugged Chambers old,
In their gloom and rudeness, hold
Dear remembrances of gold
Some first blossoming of flowers
Made delight of all the hours;
Greatness, beauty, all things fair
Made the spirit of thine air:
Old years live with thee; thy sons
Walk, with high companions.
Then, the natural joy of earth,
Joy of very health and birth!
Hills, upon a summer noon:
Water Meads, on eves of June:
Chamber Court, beneath the moon:
Days of spring, on Twyford Down,
Or when autumn woods grew brown;
As they looked, when here came Keats
Chaunting of autumnal sweets;
Through this city of old haunts,
Murmuring immortal chaunts;
As when Pope, art's earlier king,
Here, a child, did nought but sing;
Sang, a child, by nature's rule,
Round the trees of Twyford School:
Hours of sun beside Meads' Wall,
Ere the may began to fall;
Watching the rooks rise and soar,
High from lime and sycamore:
Wanderings by old-world ways,
Walks and streets of ancient days;

Closes, churches, arches, halls,
Vanished men's memorials.
There was beauty, there was grace,
Each place was an holy place:
There the kindly fates allowed
Me too room; and made me proud,
Prouder name I have not wist!
With the name of Wykehamist.
These the joys: and more than these:
Ah to watch beneath thy trees,
Through long twilights linden-scented,
Sunsets, lingering, lamented,
In the purple west; prevented,
Ere they fell, by evening star!
Ah, long nights of Winter! Far
Leaps and roars the faggot fire;
Ruddy smoke rolls higher, higher,
Broken through by flame's desire;
Circling faces flow, all eyes
Take the light; deep radiance flies,
Merrily flushing overhead
Names of brothers, long since fled;
And fresh cloisters, in their stead,
Jubilant round fierce forest flame.
Friendship too much make her claim:
But what songs, what memories end,
When they tell of friend on friend?
And for them, I thank thy name.
Love alone of gifts, no shame
Lessens, and I love thee: yet

Sound it but of echoes, let
This my maiden music be,
Of the love I bear to thee,
Witness and interpreter,
Mother mine: loved Winchester!

1888

To A Passionist

Clad in a vestment wrought with passion-flowers;
Celebrant of one Passion; called by name
Passionist: is thy world, one world with ours?
Thine, a like heart? Thy very soul, the same?

Thou pleadest an eternal sorrow: we
Praise the still changing beauty of the earth.
Passionate good and evil, thou dost see:
Our eyes behold the dreams of death and birth.

We love the joys of men: we love the dawn,
Red with the sun, and with the pure dew pearled.
Thy stern soul feels, after the sun withdrawn,
How much pain goes to perfecting the world.

Can't thou be right? Is thine the very truth?
Stands, then our life in so forlorn a state?
Nay, but thou wrongest us: thou wrong'st our youth,
Who dost our happiness compassionate.

And yet! And yet! O royal Calvary!
Whence divine sorrow triumphed through years past:
Could ages bow before mere memory?
Those passion-flowers must blossom, to the last.

Purple they bloom, the splendour of a King:
Crimson they bleed, the sacrament of Death:
About our thrones and pleasaunces they cling,
Where guilty eyes read, what each blossom saith.

1888

In a letter to Louise Imogen Guiney, dated 8th July, 1897, Lionel mentions the circumstances that inspired the poem: "In a little Passionist chapel... the celebrant had a face of beautiful austerity, and was vested in a wondrous white chasuble broidered with purple passion-flowers." For Lionel, like Oscar Wilde, Catholicism had an aesthetic appeal that verges on the decadent. Unlike Wilde, however, Johnson wasn't just interested in the mystical spectacle of the Catholic faith in the Victorian era but was a fervent believer. Oscar was to follow his contemporaries to Catholicism at the very last, finding solace in a death bed conversion. (Thank you to John Stratford, estate of Lord Alfred Douglas)

Gwynedd
To Ernest Rhys

The children of the mingling mists: can they,
Born by the melancholy hills, love thee,
Royal and joyous light? From dawn of day,
We watch the trailing shadows of the waste,
The waste moors, or the ever-mourning sea:
What, though in speedy splendour thou hast raced
Over the heather or wild wave, a ray
Of travelling glory and swift bloom? Still thou
Inhabitest the mighty morning's brow:
And hast thy flaming and celestial way,
Afar from our sad beauties, in thine haste.

Have thou thy circling triumph of the skies,
Horsemen of Goldwhite Footsteps! Yet all fire
Lives not with thee: for part is in our eyes,
Beholding the loved beauty of cold hills:
And part is patron of dear home desire,
Flashing upon the central hearth: it fills
Ingle and black-benched nook with radiances,
Hearts with responding spirit, ears with deep
Delicious music of the ruddy leap,
And steaming strength, and kindling confluences:
The hearth glows, and the cavernous chimney thrills.

Pale with great heat, panting to crimson gloom,
Quiver the deeps of the rich fire: see there!
Was not that your fair face, in burning bloom
Wrought by the art of fire? Oh happy art!
That sets in living flames a face so fair:
The face, whose changes dominate mine heart,
And with a look speak my delight or doom:
Nay, now not doom, for I am only thine,
And one in thee and me the fire divine!
The fire, that wants the whole vast world for room:
Yet dwells in us contented and apart.

The flames' red dance is done: and we crouch close
With shadowy faces to the dull, red glow.
Your darkling loveliness is like the rose,
Its dusky petals, and its bower of soft
Sweet inner darkness, where the dew lies low:
And now one tongue of flame leaps up aloft,
Brightening your brows: and now it fails, and throws
A play of flushing shadows, the rich mist
Of purple grapes, that many a sun hath kissed;
The delicate darkness, that with autumn grows
On red ripe apples in a mossy croft.

Nay! leave such idle southern imageries,
Vineyard and orchard, flowers and mellow fruit:
Great store is ours of mountain mysteries.
Look, where the embers fade, from ruddy gold
Into gray ashes, falling without bruit!
Yet is that ruddy lustre bought and sold,

Elf with elf trafficking his merchandise:
Deep at the strong foot of the eagle's pass,
They store the haunting treasure, and amass
The spirit of dead fire: there still it lies,
Phantom wealth, goodlier than Ophir old.

Across the moor, over the purple bells,
Over the heather blossom, the rain drives:
Art fired enough to dare the blowing fells,
And for the brawling brooks? Ah come we then!
Great good it is to see, how beauty thrives
For desolate moorland and for moorland men;
To smell scents, rare than soft honey cells,
From bruised wild thyme, pine bark, or mouldering peat;
Midway the ragged cliffs. O mountain spells,
Calling us forth, by hill, and moor, and glen!

Calling us forth, to be with earth again,
Her memories, her splendours, her desires!
The fires of the hearth are fallen: now the rain
Stirs its delight of waters, as the flame
Stirred its delight of heat and spirited fires.
Come by the lintel listen: clouds proclaim,
That thunder is their vast voice: the winds wane,
That all the storm may gather strength, and strive
Once more in their great breath to be alive;
And fill the angry air with such a strain,
As filled the world's war, when the world first came.

Desolate Cornwall, desolate Brittany,
Are up in vehement wind and vehement wave:
Ancient delights are on their ancient sea,
And nature's violent graces waken there;
And there goes loveliness about the grave,
And death means more than dreaming, not life's long despair.
Our sister lands are they, one people we,
Cornwall desolate, Brittany desolate,
And Wales: to us is granted to be great:
Because as winds and seas and flames are free,
We too have freedom full, as wild and rare.

And therefore, on a night of heavenly fires:
And therefore, on a windy hour of noon;
Our soul, like nature's eager soul aspires,
Finding all thunders and all winds our friends:
And like the moving sea, love we the moon;
And life in us the way of nature wends,
Ardent as nature's own, that never tires.
Born of wild land, children of mountains, we
Fear neither ruining earth, nor stormy sea:
Even as nature's own, that never tires.
Born of wild land, children of mountains, we
Fear neither running earth, nor stormy sea:
Even as men told in Athens, of our sires:
And as it shall be, till the old world ends.

Your eyes but brighten to the streaming wind,
But lighten to the sighing air, but break
To tears before the labouring hills: your mind

Moves with the passionate spirit of the land.
Now crystal is your soul, now flame: a lake,
Proud and calm, with high scaurs on either hand;
Or a swift lance of lightning, to strike blind.
True child of Gwyned, child of wilds and fields!
To you earth clings, to you strange nature yields
Far learning, sudden light, fierce fire: these find
Home in your heart, and thoughts that understand.

We will not wander from this land; we will
Be wise together, and accept our world:
This world of the gray cottage by the hill,
This gorge, this lusty air, this loneliness:
The calm of drifting clouds; the pine-tops whirled
And swayed along the ridges. Here distress
Dreams, and delight dreams: dreaming, we can fill
All solitary haunts with prophecy,
All heights with holiness and mystery;
Our hearts with understanding and our will
With love of nature's law and loveliness.

Old voices call, old pleasures lure: for now
The wet earth breathes ancient fair fragrance forth;
And dying gales hang in the branches, blow
And fall, and blow again: our widest home
Is with rich winds of West, loud winds of North
Sweeping beneath a gray and vasty dome.
Not with the hearth, whose consolations go,
Our home of homes; but where our eyes grow tired
Of straitened joys, with stretching joys are fired:

Joys of the rolling moor and cloudy brow,
Or worn, precipitous bastions of the foam.

Our fires are fallen from their blossoming height,
And linger in sad embers: but gray bloom
Is on the heather, an enchaunting light
Of purple dusk and vesper air: rich rain
Falls on our hearts, through eve and gentle gloom,
More than upon our foreheads. The world's pain
And joy of storm are proven our delight,
And peace enthroned for ever: ours the mirth,
And melancholy of this ancient earth:
Ours are the mild airs and the starred twilight;
And we who love them, are not all in vain.

1888

A fellow Rhymer, Rhys was tight with Yeats and had an interest in folklore – hence the line 'Horsemen of Goldwhite Footsteps' which has connotations with the Welsh warrior magician, Lieu Llaw Gyffes, whose steed had 'yellow-white footsteps'. Rhys founded the 'Everyman's Library' series, whose noble achievement was affordable books for all.

A Cornish Night
To William Butler Yeats

Merry the night, you riders of the wild!
A merry night to ride your wilderness.
Come you from visionary haunts, enisled
Amid the northern waters pitiless,
Over these cliffs white-heathered? Upon mild
Midnights of dewy June, oh, rare to press
Past moonlit fields of white bean flowers! nor less
To wander beside falling waves, beguiled
By soft winds into still dreams! Yet confess,
You chivalries of air, unreconciled
To the warm, breathing world! what ghostly stress
Compels your visit unto sorrow's child?

What would you here? For here you have no part:
Only the sad voices of wind and sea
Are prophets here to any wistful heart:
Or white flowers found upon a glimmering lea.
What would you here? Sweep onward, and depart
Over the sea into Brittany,
Where old faith is, and older mystery!
Though this be western land, we have no art
To welcome spirits in community:
Trafficking, in an high celestial mart,
Slumber for wondrous knowledge: setting free
Our souls, that strain and agonize and start.

The wind hath cried to me, all the long day,
That you were coming, chivalries of air!
Between the waters and the starry way.
Fair lies the sea about a land, as fair:
Moonlight and west winds move upon the bay
Gently: now down the rough path sweet it were
To clamber, and so launching out to fare
Forth for the heart of sea and night, away
From hard earth's loud uproar, and harder care!
But you at will about the winds can stray:
Or bid the wandering stars of midnight bear
You company: or with the seven stay.

And yet you came for me! So the wind cried,
So my soul knows: else why am I awake
With expectations and desire, beside
The soothed sea's murmuring nocturnal lake?
Not sleep, but storm, welcomes a widowed bride:
Storms of sad certainty, vain want, that make
Vigil perpetual mine; so that I take
The gusty night in place of him, who died,
To clasp me home to heart. That cannot break,
The eternal heart of nature far and wide!
So now, your message! While the clear stars shake
Within the gleaming sea, shake and abide.

So now, your message! Breathe words from the wave,
Or breathe words from the field, into mine ears:
Or from the sleeping shades of a cold grave

Bring comfortable solace for my tears.
Something of my love's heart could nature save:
Some rich delight to spice the tasteless years,
Some hope to light the valley of lone fears.
Hear! I am left alone, to bear and brave
The sounding storms: but you, from starry spheres,
From wild wood haunts, give me, as love once gave
Joy from his home celestial, so, love's peers!
Give peace awhile to me, sorrow's poor slave!

In sorrow's order I dwell passionist,
Cloistered by tossing sea on weary land.
O vain love! vain, to claim me votarist:
O vain my heart! That will not understand,
He is dead! I am lonely! Love in a Mist
My flower is: and salt tangle of the strand,
The crownals woven by this failing hand:
In the dark kingdom, walking where I list,
I walk where Lethe glides against the sand.
But vain love is a constant lutanist,
Playing old airs, and able to withstand
Sweet sleep: vain love, thou loyal melodist!

You wanderers! Would I were wandering
Under the white moon with you, or among
The invisible stars with you! Would I might sing
Over the charmed sea your enchaunting song,
Song of old autumn, and of radiant spring:
Might sing, how earth the mother suffers long;

How the great winds are wild, yet do no wrong;
How the most frail bloom is at heart a king!
I could endure then, strenuous and strong:
But now, O spirits of the air! I bring
Before you my waste soul: why will you throng
About me, save to take even such a thing?

Only for this you ride the midnight gloom,
Above the ancient isles of the old main.
The spray leaps on the hidden rocks of doom:
The ripples break, and wail away again
Upon the gathering wave: gaunt headlands loom
In the lone distance of the heaving plain
And now, until the calm, the still stars wane,
You wait upon my heart, my heart a tomb.
Though I dream, life and dreams are alike vain!
Then love me, tell me news of dear death: whom
Circle you, but a soul astray, one fain
To leave this close world for death's larger room?

If barren be the promise I desire,
The promise that I shall not always go
In living solitariness: break fire
Out of the night, and lay me swiftly low!
Soft spirits! You have wings to waft me higher,
Than touch of each my most familiar woe:
Am I unworthy, you should raise me so?
If barren be that trust, my dreams inspire
Only despair: my brooding heart must grow

Heavy with miseries; a mourning quire,
To tell the heavy hours, how sad, how slow,
Are all their footsteps, of whose sound I tire.
Bright sea fire runs about a plunging keel
On vehement nights: and where black danger lies,
Gleam the torn breakers. But all days reveal
Drear dooms for me, nor any nights disguise
Their menace: never rolls the thunder peal
Through my worn watch, nor lightning past mine eyes
Leaps from the blue gloom of its mother skies,
One hour alone, but all, while sad stars wheel.
This hour, was it a lie, that bade me rise;
Some laughing dream, that whispered me to steal
Into the sea-sweet night, where the wind cries,
And find the comfort, that I cannot feel?

My lord hath gone your way perpetual:
Whether you be great spirits of the dead,
Or spirits you, that never were in thrall
To perishing bodies, dust-born, dustward led.
Sweet shadows! Passing by this ocean wall,
Tarry to pour some balm upon mine head,
Some pity for a woman, who hath wed
With weariness and loneliness, from fall
To fall, from bitter snows to maybloom red:
The hayfields hear, the cornlands hear, my call!
From weariness toward weariness I tread;
And hunger for the end: the end of all.

1888

By the Statue of King Charles At Charing Cross
To William Watson

Sombre and rich, the skies;
Great glooms, and starry plains.
Gently the night wind sighs;
Else a vast silence reigns.

The splendid silence clings
Around me: and around
The saddest of all kings
Crowned, and again discrowned.

Comely and calm, he rides
Hard by his own Whitehall:
Only the night wind glides:
No crowds, nor rebels, brawl.

Gone, too his Court: and yet,
The stars his courtiers are:
Stars in their stations set;
And every wandering star.

Alone he rides, alone,
The fair and fatal king:
Dark night is all his own,
That strange and solemn thing.

Which are more full of fate:
The stars; or those sad eyes?
Which are more still and great:
Those brows; or the dark skies?

Although his whole heart yearn
In passionate tragedy:
Never was face so stern
With sweet austerity.

Vanquished in life, his death
By beauty made amends:
The passing of his breath
Won his defeated ends.

Brief life, and hapless? Nay:
Through death, life grew sublime.
Speak after sentence? Yea:
And to the end of time.

Armoured he rides, his head
Bare to the stars of doom:
He triumphs now, the dead,
Beholding London's gloom.

Our wearier spirit faints,
Vexed in the world's employ:
His soul was of the saints;
And art to him was joy.

King, tried in fires of woe!
Men hunger for thy grace:
And through the night I go,
Loving thy mournful face.

Yet, when the city sleeps;
When all the cries are still:
The stars and heavenly deeps
Work out a perfect will.

1889

Lionel summarised Watson's poetry in an 1895 letter to Katharine Tynan, noting: "At his best, he impresses by his frequent stateliness and purity of phrase." Clearly, then, he was an influence on Johnson.

Beyond

All was for you: and you are dead.
For, came there sorrow, came there splendour,
You still were mine, and I yours only:
Then on my breast lay down your head,
Triumphant in its dear surrender:
One were we then: though one, not lonely.

Oh, is it you are dead, or I?
Both! both dead, since we are asunder:
You, sleeping: I for ever walking
Through the dark valley, hard and dry.
At times I hear the mourning thunder:
And voices, in the shadows, talking.

Dear, are there dreams among the dead:
Or is it all a perfect slumber?
But I must dream and dream to madness.
Mine eyes are dark, now yours are fled.
Yet see they sorrows without number,
Waiting upon one perfect sadness.

So long, the melancholy vale!
So full, these weary winds, of sorrow!
So harsh, all things! For what counts pity?
Still, as each twilight glimmers pale
Upon the borders of each morrow,
I near me to your sleeping city.

1889

A Dream of Youth
For Lord Alfred Douglas

With faces bright, as ruddy corn,
Touched by the sunlight of the morn;
With rippling hair; and gleaming eyes,
Wherein a sea of passion lies;
Hair waving back, and eyes that gleam
With deep delight of dream on dream;
With full lips, curving into song;
With shapely limbs, upright and strong:
The youths on holy service throng.

Vested in white, upon their brows
Are wreaths fresh twined from dewy boughs:
And flowers they strow along the way,
Still dewy from the birth of day.
So, to each revered altar come,
They stand in adoration: some
Swing up gold censers; till the air
Is blue and sweet, with smoke of rare
Spices, that fetched from Egypt were.

In voices of calm, choral tone,
Praise they each God, with praise his own:
As children of the Gods, is seen
Their glad solemnity of mien:
So fair a spirit of the skies
Is in their going: and their eyes
Look out upon the peopled earth.

As theirs were some diviner birth:
And clear and courtly is their mirth.

Lights of the labouring world, they seem:
Or, to the tired, like some fresh stream.
Their dignity of perfect youth
Compels devotion, as doth truth:
So right seems all, they do, they are.
Old age looks wistful, from afar,
To watch their beauty, as they go,
Radiant and free, in ordered row;
And fairer, in the watching, grow

Fair though it be, to watch unclose
The nestling glories of a rose,
Depth on rich depth, soft fold on fold:
Though fairer be it, to behold
Stately and sceptral lilies break
To beauty, and to sweetness wake:
Yet fairer still, to see and sing,
One fair thing is, one matchless thing:
Youth, in its perfect blossoming.

The magic of a golden grace
Brings fire and sweetness on each face:
Till, from their passage, every heart
Takes fire, and sweetness in the smart:
Till virtue lives, for all who own
Their majesty, in them alone:

Till careless hearts, and idle, take
Delight in living, for their sake;
Worship their footsteps, and awake.

Beside the tremulous, blue sea,
Clear at sunset, they love to be:
And they are rarely sad, but then.
For sorrow touches them, as men,
Looking upon the calm of things,
That pass, and wake rememberings
Of holy and of ancient awe;
The charm of immemorial Law:
What we see now, the great dead saw!

Upon a morn of storm, a swan,
Breasting the cold stream, cold and wan,
Throws back his neck in snowy length
Between his snowy wings of strength:
Against him the swift river flows,
The proudlier he against it goes,
King of the waters! For his pride
Bears him upon a mightier tide:
May death not be by youth defied!

But the red sun is gone: and gleams
Of delicate moonlight waken dreams,
Dreams, and the mysteries of peace:
Shall this fair darkness never cease?
Here is no drear, no fearful Power,

But life grows fuller with each hour,
Full of the silence, that is best:
Earth lies, with soothed and quiet breast,
Beneath the guardian stars, at rest.

At night, behold them! Where lights burn
By moonlit olives, see them turn
Full faces toward the sailing moon,
Night lovelier than beneath high noon!
Throw back their comely moulded throats,
Whence music on the night wind floats!
And through the fragrant hush of night
Their lustrous eyes make darkness bright:
Their laugh loads darkness with delight.

Almost the murmuring sea is still:
Almost the world obeys their will.
Such youth moves pity in stern Fates,
And sure death wellnigh dominates:
Their passion kindles such fair flame,
As from divine Achilles came:
A vehement ardour thrills their breasts,
And beauty's benediction rests
On earth, and on earth's goodliest guests.

The music of their sighing parts
A silence: and their beating hearts
Beat to a measure of despair:
Ah! How the fire of youth is fair,

Yet may not be forever young!
But night hath yielded, there hath sprung
Morning upon the throne of night:
Day comes, with solemnizing light:
Consuming sorrows take to flight.

Magnificent in early bloom,
Like Gods, they triumph over gloom:
All things desirable are theirs,
Of beauty and of wonder, heirs:
Their cities, vassals are, which give
Them thanks and praise, because they live:
Strong, they are victors of dismay;
Fair, they serve beauty every day;
Young, the sun loves to light their way.

Where now is death? Where that gray land?
Those fearless eyes, those white brows grand,
That take full sunlight and sweet air
With rapture true and debonair,
These have not known the touch of death!
The world hath winds: these forms have breath.
But should death come, should dear life set,
Calm would each go: *Farewell! Forget
Me dead: live you serenely yet.*

See them! The springing of the palm
Is nought beside their gracious calm:
The rippling of cool waters dies

To nought, before their clear replies:
The smile, that heralds their bright thought,
Brings down the splendid sun to nought.
See them! They walk the earth in state:
In right of perfect youth, held great:
On whom the powers of nature wait.

No sceptre theirs, but they are kings:
Their forms and words are royal things.
Their simple friendship is a court,
Whither the wise and great resort.
No homage of the world, they claim:
But in all places lives their fame.
Sun, moon, and stars; the earth, the sea;
Yea! All things, that of beauty be,
Honour their true divinity.

1889

Lines to a Lady Upon Her Third Birthday

Dear Cousin: to be three years old,
Is to have found the Age of Gold:
That Age forgone! That Age foretold!
What wondrous names, then, wait thy choice,
High sounding for thine helpless voice!
I choose instead: and hail in thee
A queen of lilied Arcady,
Or lady of Hesperides:
Or if Utopia lie near these,
Utopian thou, by right divine,
On whom all stars of favour shine.
Vainly the cold Lycean sage
Withheld his praise from childhood's age;
Denied thine happiness to thee;
Nor as a little child would be!
Man to the world he could present,
Magnanimous, magnificent:
Children, he knew not: for of thee
Dreamed not his calm philosophy;
Or Pythias was no Dorothy!
Thou has good right to laugh in scorn
At us, of simple dreams forlorn:
At us, whose disenchaunted eyes
Imagination dare despise.
Thou hast that freshness, early born,
Which roses have; or billowy corn,
Waving and washed in dews of morn:

And yet, no flower of woodlands wild,
But overwhelming London's child!
About thy sleep are heard the feet
And turmoil of the sounding street:
Thou hearest not! The land of dreams
More closely lies, and clearlier gleams.
Thou watchest, with thy grave eyes gray,
Our world, with looks of far away:
Eyes that consent to look on things
Unlike their own imaginings;
And looking, weave round all they see,
Charms of their own sweet sorcery.
Thus very London thou dost change
To wonderland, all fair and strange:
The ugliness and uproar seem
To soften, at a child's pure dream:
And each poor dusty garden yields
The fresh delight of cowslip fields.
What is the secret, and the spell?
Thou knowest: for thou has it well.
Wilt thou not teach us, how to make
Worlds of delight from things of nought,
Or fetched from faery land, and wrought
With flowers and lovely imageries?
Pity us! for such wisdom dies:
Pity thyself! youth flies, youth flies.
Thou comest to the desert plain,
Where no dreams follow in thy train:
They leave thee at the pleasaunce close;

Lonely the haggard pathway goes.
Thou wilt look back, and see them, deep
In the fair glades, where thou didst keep
Thy summer court, thy summer sleep:
But thou wilt never see them more,
Till death the golden dreams restore.
Now, ere the hard, dull hours begin
Their sad destroying work within
Thy childhood's delicate memory,
Wilt thou not tell us, Dorothy?
Nay! thou art in conspiracy
With all those faeries, children styled,
To keep the secret of the child.
Ah to be only three years old!
That is indeed an Age of Gold:
And care not for mine idle fears!
Thou need'st not lose it: the far years,
Touching with love and gentle tears
The treasures of thy memory,
May mould them into poetry.
Then, of those deep eyes, gray and grave,
The world will be a willing slave:
Then, all the dreams of dear dreamland
Wait with their music at thine hand,
And beauty come at thy command.
But now, what counts the will of time?
Enough, thou livest! And this rhyme,
Unworthy of the Golden Age,
Yet hails thee, in that heritage,

Happy and fair: then, come what may,
Thou hast the firstfruits of the day.
Fair fall each morn to thee! And I,
Despite all dark fates, Dorothy!
Will prove me thine affectionate
Cousin, and loyal Laureate.

1889

A poem dedicated to Dorothy Shakespear, the daughter of Lionel's cousin Olivia. In 1915, Dorothy edited the first collection of Lionel's poetry. She was to also suffer a marriage to Ezra Pound.

Trentals
To Charles Sayle

Now these lovers twain be dead,
And together buried:
Masses only shall be said.
Hush thee, weary melancholy!
Music comes, more rich and holy:
Through the aged church shall sound
Words, by ancient prophets found;
Burdens in an ancient tongue,
By the fasting Mass-priest sung.

Gray, without, the autumn air:
But pale candles here prepare,
Pale as wasted golden hair.
Let the quire with mourning descant
Cry: *In pace requiescant!*
For they loved the things of God.
Now, where solemn feet have trod,
Sleep they well: and wait the end,
Lover by lover, friend by friend.

1889

One of Lionel's Winchester correspondents, Charles Sayle (1864-1924) worked as an Assistant Librarian at the University Library, Cambridge and was a published poet.

Bagley Wood
To Percy Addleshaw

The night is full of stars, full of magnificence:
Nightingales hold the wood, and fragrance loads the
　　dark.
Behold, what fires august, what lights eternal! Hark,
What passionate music poured in passionate love's
　　defence!
Breathe but the wafting wind's nocturnal frankincense!
　　Only to feel this night's great heart, only to mark
The splendours and the glooms, brings back the
　　patriarch
Who on Chaldean wastes found God through reverence.

Could we but live at will upon this perfect height,
Could we but always keep the passion of this peace,
Could we but face unshamed the look of this pure light,
Could we but win earth's heart and give desire release:
Then were we all divine, and then were ours by right
These stars, these nightingales, these scents: then
　　shame would cease.

1890

Lionel's friend from Oxford and an habitué of the Crown in
Charing Cross, William Percy Addleshaw turned his hand to
poetry, penning *The Happy Wanderer and other Verse* (1896) and
Lost Verses (1920) which includes a biographical memoir.

The Age of a Dream
To Christopher Whall

Imageries of dreams reveal a gracious age:
Black armour, falling lace, and altar lights at morn.
The courtesy of Saints, their gentleness and scorn,
Lights on an earth more fair, than shone from Plato's page:
The courtesy of knights, fair calm and sacred rage:
The courtesy of love, sorrow for love's sake borne.
Vanished, those high conceits! Desolate and forlorn,
We hunger against hope for that lost heritage.

Gone now, the carven work! Ruined, the golden shrine!
No more the glorious organs pour their voice divine;
No more rich frankincense drifts through the Holy Place:
Now from the broken tower, what solemn bell still tolls,
Mourning what piteous death? Answer, O saddened souls!
Who mourn the death of beauty and the death of grace.

1890

Christopher Whall was an accomplished stained glass artist,
whose work graces the Chapter House, in Gloucester Cathedral.

The Church of a Dream
To Bernhard Berenson

Sadly the dead leaves rustle in the whistling wind,
Around the weather-worn, gray church, low down the vale:
The Saints in golden vesture shake before the gale;
The glorious windows shake, where still they dwell
     enshrined;
Old Saints by long dead, shrivelled hands, long since
     designed:
There still, although the world autumnal be, and pale,
Still in their golden vesture the old saints prevail;
Alone with Christ, desolate else, left by mankind.

Only one ancient Priest offers the Sacrifice,
Murmuring holy Latin immemorial:
Swaying with tremulous hands the old censer full of spice,
In gray, sweet incense clouds; blue, sweet clouds, mystical:
To him, in place of men, for he is old, suffice
Melancholy remembrances and vesperal.

1890

Bernhard Berenson was a highly regarded art historian and specialist in Italian paintings.

In Honorem Doriani Creatorisque Eius

Benedictus sis, Oscare!
Qui me libro hoc dignare
   Proper amicitias:
Modo modulans Romano
Laudes dignas Doriano,
    Ago tibi gratias.

Juventutis hic Formosa
Floret inter rosa rosa
   Subito dum venit mors:
Ecce Homo! ecce Deus!
Si sic modo esset meus
    Genius mesericors!

Amat avidus amores
Miros, miros carpit flores
   Saevus pulchritudine:
Quanto anima nigrescit,
Tanto facies splendescit,
   Mendax, sed quam splendide!

Hic sunt poma Sodomorum;
Hic sunt corda vitiorium;
   Et peccata dulcia.
In excelsis et infernis,
Tibi sit, qui tanta cernis,
    Gloriarum gloria.

In Honour of Dorian and his Creator

Blessed be you, Oscar! Who deem me worthy of this book For friendship's sake. Modulating in the Roman mode Praises to the Dorian owed, I give you thanks. Here the lovely rose Flourishes amid the roses When suddenly comes death: Behold the Man! Behold the God! O that this mode of pitying Genius were but mine! Avidly he loves strange loves, Savage with beauty Plucks strange flowers: The more his soul is darkened, His face displays its brightness more, False, but how radiantly so! Here are apples of Sodom; Here the hearts of vices; And sweet sins. In the heavens and in the depths, Be to you, who perceive so much, Glory of all glories.

1891

'In Honorem' was not published during Lionel's lifetime. It first appeared in print in *Art and Morality* by Stuart Mason (Christopher Millard) in 1912.

To Morfydd

A voice on the winds,
A voice by the waters,
    Wanders and cries:
Oh! what are the winds?
And what are the waters?
    Mine are your eyes!

Western the winds are,
And western the waters,
    Where the light lies:
Oh! what are the winds?
And what are the waters?
    Mine are your eyes!

Cold, cold, grow the winds,
And wild grow the waters,
    Where the sun dies:
Oh! what are the winds!
And what are the waters?
    Mine are your eyes!

And down the night winds,
And down the night waters,
    The music flies:

Oh! what are the winds?
And what are the waters?
Cold be the winds,
And wild be the waters,
    So mine be your eyes!

1891

The Destroyer of A Soul
For Oscar Wilde

I hate you with a necessary hate.
First, I sought patience: passionate was she:
My patience turned in very scorn of me,
That I should dare forgive a sin so great,
As this, through which I sit disconsolate;
Mourning for that live soul, I used to see;
Soul of a saint, whose friend I used to be:
Till you came by! A cold, corrupting, fate.

Why come you now? You, whom I cannot cease
With pure and perfect hate to hate? Go, ring
The death-bell with a deep, triumphant toll!
Say you, my friend sits by me still? Ah peace!
Call you this thing my friend? This nameless thing?
This living body, hiding its dead soul?

1892

Vinum Daemonum
To Stephen Phillips

The crystal fame, the ruby flame,
Alluring, dancing, revelling!
See them: and ask me not, whence came
      This cup I bring.

But only watch the wild wine glow,
But only taste its fragrance: then,
Drink the wild drink I bring, and so
      Reign among men.

Only one sting, and then but joy:
One pang of fire, and thou art free.
Then, what thou wilt, thou canst destroy:
      Save only me!

Triumph in tumult of thy lust:
Wanton in passion of thy will:
Cry Peace! to conscience, and it must
      At last be still

I am the Prince of this World: I
Command the flames, command the fires.
Mine are the draughts, that satisfy
      This World's desires.

Thy longing leans across the brink:
Ah, the brave thirst within thine eyes!
For there is that within this drink,
      Which never dies.

1893

The actor and poet, Stephen Phillips, (1864-1915) allegedly shared
Lionel's unfortunate predilection for drink.

The Precept of Silence

I know you: solitary griefs,
Desolate passions, aching hours!
I know you: tremulous beliefs,
Agonized hopes, and ashen flowers!

The winds are sometimes sad to me;
The starry spaces, full of fear:
Mine is the sorrow of the sea,
And mine the sigh of places drear.

Some players upon plaintive strings
Publish their wistfulness abroad:
I have not spoken of these things,
Save to one man, and unto God.

1893

Ash Wednesday
To the Rev. Father Strappini, S.J.

Ashen cross traced on brow!
Iron cross hid in breast!
Have power, bring patience, now:
Bid passion be at rest.

O sad, dear, days of Lent!
Now lengthen your gray hours:
If so we may repent,
Before the time of flowers.

Majestical, austere,
The sanctuaries look stern:
All silent! all severe!
Save where the lone lamps burn.

Imprisoned there above
The world's indifferency:
Still waits Eternal Love,
With wounds from Calvary.

Come! Mourning companies;
Come! To sad Christ draw near:
Come! sin's confederacies;
Lay down your malice here.

Here is the healing place,
And here the place of peace:
Sorrow is sweet with grace
Here, and here sin hath cease.

1893

Fr. Walter Strappini, S.J. (1849-1914) was in residence at Oxford, whilst Lionel was a student.

Ireland

To Mrs. Clement Shorter

Si oblitus fuero tui Ierusalem: oblivioni detur dextera mea

Thy sorrow, and the sorrow of the sea,
Are sisters; the sad winds are of thy race
The heart of melancholy beats in thee,
And the lamenting spirit haunts thy face,
Mournful and mighty Mother! who art kin
      To the ancient earth's first woe,
When holy Angels wept, beholding sin.
For not in penance do thy true tears flow,
Not thine the long transgression: at thy name,
      We sorrow not with shame,
But proudly: for thy soul is as the snow.

Old as the sorrow for lost Paradise
Seems thine old sorrow: thou in the mild West,
Who woulds't thy children upon earth suffice
For Paradise, and pure Hesperian rest;
Had not the violent and bitter fates
      Burned up with fiery feet
The greenness of thy pastures; had not hates,
Envies, and desolations, with fierce heat
Wasted thee, and consumed the land of grace,
      Beauty's abiding place;
And vexed with agony's bright joy's retreat.
Swift at the word of the Eternal Will,
Upon thee the malign armed Angels came.

Flame was their winging, flame that laps thee still;
And in the anger of their eyes was flame,
One was the Angel of the field of blood,
      And one of lonelier death:
One saddened exiles on the ocean flood,
And famine followed on another's breath.
Angels of evil, with incessant sword,
      Smote thee, O land adored!
And yet smite: for the will of God so saith.

A severing and sundering they wrought,
A rending of the soul. They turned to tears
The laughter of thy waters: and they brought,
To sow upon thy fields, quick seed of fears;
That brother should hate brother, and one roof
      Shelter unkindly hearts;
Friend from his ancient friendship hold aloof,
And comrades learn to play sad alien parts;
Province from noble province dwell estranged,
      And all old trusts be changed;
And treason teach true men her impious arts.

But yet in their reluctant hands they bore
Laurel, and palm, and crown, and bay: an host,
Heartened by wrath and sorrow more and more,
Strove ever, giving up the mighty ghost;
The field well fought, the song well sung, for sake,
      Mother! of thee alone:
Sorrow and wrath bade deathless courage wake,
And struck from burning harps a deathless tone.

With palm and laurel won, with crown and bay,
        Went proudly down death's way
Children of Ireland, to their deathless throne.

Proud and sweet habitation of thy dead!
Throne upon throne, its throne of sorrow filled;
Prince on prince coming with triumphant tread,
All passion, save the love of Ireland, stilled.
By the forgetful waters they forget
        Not thee, O Inisfail!
Upon thy fields their dreaming eyes are set,
They hear thy winds call ever through each vale.
Visions of victory exalt and thrill
        Their hearts' whole hunger still:
High beats their longing for the living Gael.

Sarsfield is sad there with his last desire;
Fitzgerald mourns with Emmet; ancient chiefs
Dream on their saffron-mantled hosts, afire
Against the givers of their Mother's griefs.
Was it for nought, captain asks captain old,
        Was it in vain, we fell?
Shall we have fallen like the leaves of gold,
And no green spring wake from the long dark spell?
Shall never a crown of summer fruitage come
        From blood of martyrdom?
Yet to our faith will we not say farewell!

There the white soul of Davis, there the worn,
Waste soul of Mangan, there the surging soul
Of Grattan, hunger for thy promised morn:
There the great legion of thy martyr roll,
Filled with the fames of seven hundred years,
      Hunger to hear the voice,
Sweeter than marriage music in their ears,
That shall bid thee and all thy sons rejoice.
There bide the spirits, who for the yet burn:
      Ah! might we but return,
And make once more for thee the martyr choice!

No swordsmen are the Christians! Oisin cried:
O Patrick! thine is but a little race.
Nay, ancient Oisin! they have greatly died
In battle glory and with warrior grace.
Signed with the Cross, they conquered and they fell:
      Sons of the Cross, they stand:
The Prince of Peace love righteous warfare well,
And loves thine armies, O our Holy Land!
The Lord of Hosts is with thee, and thine eyes
      Shall see upon thee rise
His glory and the blessing of His Hand.

Thou hast no fear: with immemorial pride,
Bright as when Oscar ran the morning glades;
The knightly Fenian hunters at his side,
The sunlight through green leaves glad on their blades;
The heart in thee is full of joyous faith.
      Not in the bitter dust

Thou crouchest, heeding what the coward saith:
But, radiant with an everlasting trust,
Hearest thine ancient rivers in their glee
    Sing themselves on to sea,
Thy winds make melody: O joy most just!

Nay! we insult thee not with tears, although
With thee we sorrow: not as for one dead
We mourn, for one in the cold earth laid low.
Still is the crown upon thy sovereign head,
Still is the screptre within thy strong hand,
    Still is the kingdom thine:
The armies of thy sons on thy command
Wait, and thy starry eyes through darkness shine.
Tears for the dear and dead! For thee, *All Hail!*
    Unconquered Inisfail!
Tears for the lost: thou livest, O divine!

Thou passest not away: the sternest powers
Spoil not all beauty of thy face, nor mar
All peace of thy great heart, O pulse of ours!
The darkest cloud dims thee not all, O star!
Ancient and proud thy sorrows, and their might
    That of the murmuring waves:
They hearten us to fight the unceasing fight,
Filled with the grave, that flows from holy graves.
Sons pass away, and thou hast sons as true
    To fight the fight anew:
Thy welfare, all the gain their warfare craves.
Sweet Mother! in what marvellous dear ways

Close to thine heart thou keepest all thine own!
Far off, they yet can consecrate their days
To thee, and on the swift winds westward blown,
Send thee the homage of their hearts, their vow
      Of one most sacred care;
To thee devote all passionate power, since thou
Vouchsafest them, O land of love! to bear
Sorrow and joy with thee. Each far son thrills
      Toward thy blue dreaming hills,
And longs to kiss thy feet upon them, Fair!

If death come swift upon me, it will be
Because of the great love I bear the Gael!
So sang upon the separating sea
Columba, while his boat sped out of hail,
And all grew lonely. But some sons thou hast,
      Whose is an heavier lot,
Close at thy side: they see thy torment last,
And all their will to help thee helps thee not.
Mother! their grief, to look on thy dear face,
      Worn with every weary trace
Of fresh woes, and of old woes unforgot!

And yet great spirits ride thy winds: thy ways
Are haunted and enchaunted evermore.
Thy children hear the voices of old days
In music of the sea upon thy shore,
In falling of the waters from thine hills,
      In whispers of thy trees:
A glory from the things eternal fills

Their eyes, and at high noon thy people see
Visions, and wonderful is all the air.
  So upon earth they share
Eternity: they learn it at thy knees.

Eternal is our faith in thee: the sun
Shall sooner fall from Heaven, than from our lives
That faith; and the great stars fade one by one,
Ere fade that light in which thy people strives.
Strong in the everlasting righteousness
  Triumphs our faith: the fight
Hath holiest hosts to inspire it and to bless;
Thy children lift true faces to the light.
Theirs are the visitations from on high,
  Voices that call and cry:
Celestial comfort in the deep of night.

Charmed upon waters three, forlorn and cold,
The swans, Children of Lir, endured their doom:
From off their white wings flashed the morning gold,
And round their white wings closed the twilight gloom.
Yet on their stormy weird the Christian bell
Broke, and they stirred with dread:
The Coming of the Saints upon them fell;
They woke to joy, and found their white wings fled.
And thou, in these last days, shalt thou not hear
  A sound of sacred fear?
God's bells shall ring, and all sad days be dead.

But desolate be the houses of thy foes:
Sorrow encompass them, and vehement wrath
Besiege them: be their hearts cold as the snows:
Let lamentation keen about their path.
The fires of God burn round them, and His night
       Lie on their blinded eyes:
And when they call to their Eternal Light,
None shall make answer to their stricken cries.
Mercy and pity shall not know them more:
       God shall shut to the door,
And close on them His everlasting skies.

How long? Justice of Very God! How long?
The Isle of Sorrows from of old hath trod
The stony road of unremitting wrong,
The purple winepress of the wrath of God:
Is then the Isle of Destiny indeed
       To grief predestinate;
Ever foredoomed to agonize and bleed,
Beneath the scourging of eternal fate?
Yet against hope shall we still hope, and still
       Beseech the Eternal Will:
Our lives to this one service dedicate.

Ah, tremble into passion, Harp! and sing
War song, O Sword! Fill the fair land, great Twain!
Wake all her heavy heart to triumphing:
To vengeance, and armed trampling of the plain!
And you, white spirits on the mountain wind,
       Cry between eve and morn!

Cry, mighty Dead! until the people find
Their souls a furnace of desire and scorn.
Call to the hosting upon Tara, call
      The tribes of Eire all:
Trump of the Champions! immemorial Horn!

Shall not the Three Waves thunder for their King,
The Captain of thy people? Shall not streams
Leap from thy mountains' heart, and many a spring
Gladden thy valleys, for the joy of dreams
      Hast thou no prophet left?
Is all thy Druid wizardry undone,
And thou of thy foreknowledge quite bereft?
Nay! but the power of faith is prophecy,
      Vision and certainty:
Faith, that hath walked the waves, and mountain cleft.

As haunting Tirnanoge within the sea,
So hid within the Eyes of God thy fate
Lies dreaming: and when God shall bid it be,
Ah, then the fair perfection of thy state!
Bravely the gold and silver bells shall chime,
      When thou art wed with peace:
Far to the desert of their own sad clime
Shall fly the ill Angels, when God bids them cease.
Thine shall be only a majestic joy,
      No evil can destroy:
The sorrows of thy soul shall have release.

Thy blood of martyrs to the martyrs' Home
Cries from the earth: the altar of high Heaven
Is by their cries besieged and overcome:
The Rainbow Throne and flaming Spirits Seven
Know well the music of that agony,
        That surge of a long sigh,
That voice of an unresting misery,
That ardour of anguish unto the Most High.
Thou from thy wronged earth pleadest with the Just,
        Whose loving-mercy must
Hear, and command thy death in life to die.

Golden allies are thine, bright souls of Saints,
Glad choirs of intercession for the Gael:
Their flame of prayer ascends, for their stream of plaints
Flows to the wounded Feet, for Inisfail.
Victor, the Angel of thy Patrick, pleads;
        Mailed Michael with his sword
Kneels there, the champion of thy bitter needs,
Prince of the shining armies of the Lord:
And there, Star of the Morning and the Sea,
        Mary pours prayers for thee:
And unto Mary be thy prayers outpoured.

O Rose! O Lily! O Lady full of grace!
O Mary Mother! O Mary Maid! hear thou.
Glory of Angels! Pity, and turn thy face,
Praying for thy Son, even as we pray thee now,
For thy dear sake to set thine Ireland free:
        Pray thou they little Child!

Ah! who can help her, but in mercy He?
Pray then, pray thou for Ireland, Mother mild!
O Heart of Mary! pray the Sacred Heart:
    His at Whose word depart
Sorrows and hates, home to Hell's waste and wild.

1894

Mrs. Clement Shorter, née Dora Sigerson, was a patriotic Irish poet who was said to have died of grief after the failure of the Easter Uprising. She also rhymed upon Irish folklore and legend, which is reflected in the poem; 'The Children of Lir' being especially poignant in the canon of Celtic folktales. Johnson regarded Ireland as his mystical motherland and though he frequently waxed lyrical in verse over his adopted country, this particular poem is his most epic.

The Dark Angel

Dark Angel, with thine aching lust
To rid the world of penitence:
Malicious Angel, who still dost
My soul such subtile violence!

Because of thee, no thought, no thing,
Abides for me undesecrate:
Dark Angel, ever on the wing,
Who never reaches me too late!

When music sounds, then changest thou
Its silvery to a sultry fire:
Nor will thine envious heart allow
Delight untortured by desire.

Through thee, the gracious Muses turn
To Furies, O mine Enemy!
And all the things of beauty burn
With flames of evil ecstasy.

Because of thee, the land of dreams
Becomes a gathering place of fears:
Until tormented slumber seems
One vehemence of useless tears.

When sunlight glows upon the flowers,
Or ripples down the dancing sea:
Thou, with thy troop of passionate powers,
Beleagurest, bewilderest, me.

Within the breath of autumn woods,
Within the winter silences:
Thy venomous spirit stirs and broods,
O Master of impieties!

The ardour of red flame is thine,
And thine the steely soul of ice:
Thou poisonest the fair design
Of nature, with unfair device.

Apples of Ashes, golden bright;
Waters of bitterness, how sweet!
O banquet of a foul delight,
Prepared by thee, dark Paraclete!

Thou art the whisper in the gloom,
The hinting tone, the haunting laugh:
Thou art the adorner of my tomb,
The minstrel of mine epitaph.

I fight thee, in the Holy Name!
Yet, what thou dost, is what God saith:
Tempter! Should I escape thy flame,
Thou will have helped my soul from Death:

The second Death, that never dies,
That cannot die, when time is dead:
Live Death, wherein the lost soul cries,
Eternally uncomforted.

Dark Angel, with thine aching lust!
Of two defeats, of two despairs:
Less dread, a change to drifting dust,
Than thine eternity of cares.

Do what thou wilt, thou shalt not so,
Dark Angel! triumph over me:
Lonely, unto the Lone I go;
Divine, to the Divinity.

1893

Flos Florum
To Mrs. Hinkson

Lily, O Lily of the Vallies!
Lily, O Lily of Calvary Hill!
White with the glory of all graces,
Earth with the breath of thy pure soul fill:
Lily, O Lily of the Vallies!
Lily, O Lily of Calvary Hill!

Rose, O Rose of Gethsemani Garden!
Rose of the Paradise: Mystical Rose!
From thickets of the thornless Eden,
Load with rich odour each wind that blows:
Rose, O Rose of Gethsemani Garden!
Rose of the Paradise: Mystical Rose!

1894

Irish author, Katharine Tynan, who married barrister, Henry Hinkson, chronicled her friendship with both Lionel and Louise Imogen Guiney, in a volume entitled *Memories* (1924, Everleigh Nash & Grayson).

Satanas
To Jorge Santayana

Ecce! Princeps infernorium.
Rex veneficus amorum
Vilium et mortiferorium,
  Ecce! Regnat Lucifer:
Animis qui dominator,
Quibus coelom spoliatur;
Qui malignus bona fatur,
  Cor corrumoebs suaviter.

Fructus profert; inest cinis:
Profer flores plenos spinis:
Vitae eius mors est finis:
  Crux est eisus requies.
Qualis illic apparebit
Cruciatus, et manebit!
Quantas ista quot habebit
  Mors amaritudines!

Iuventutis quam Formosa
Florest inter rosas rosa!
Venit autem vitiosa
  Species infamiae:
Veniunt crudeles visus,
Voces simulate risus;
Et inutilis fit nisus
  Flebilis laetitiae.

Quanto vitium splendescit,
Tanto anima nigrescit;
Tanto tandem cor marcescit,
  Per oeccata dulcia.
Gaudens mundi Princeps mali
Utitur veneno tali,
Voluptate Avernali;
 O melita vitia!

Gaudet Princeps huius mundi
Videns animam confundi;
Cordis amat moribundi
  Aspectare proelium.
Vana tentat, vana quarens,
Cor anhelum, frusta moerens;
Angit animae inhaerens
  Flamma cor miserrimum.

Gaudet Rector tenebrarum
Immolare cor amarum;
Satiare furiarum
  Rex sorores avidas
Vae! non stabit in aeternum
Regnum, ait Rex, infernum:
Sed, dum veniat Supernum,
  Dabo Vobis victimas.

1893

Satanas

Behold! The Prince of Hell, Venomous King of cheap And Death-bearing love, Lo! Lucifer reigns: He who rules over souls, Of whom Heaven is plundered; He who speaks good with ill intention, Corrupting the heart with sweetness. He offers fruits; there are ashes in them: He offers flowers full of thorns: Death is the purpose of his life: The cross his resting place. How tormented shall he appear there, And thus shall he remain! How many bitternesses Shall that death have! How fair amid the roses Flourishes the lovely rose of youth! When lo! comes the ruinous shape of infamy: The cruel faces appear, The voices of dissimulated laughter; And vain the pathetic effort Towards joy. As vice glisters the more, So the soul is tarnished more; And the heart withers at last, Through delicious sins. Rejoicing the Prince of the world of evil Uses poisons of such kind, Carnalities of Hell; Oh honeyed vices! The Prince of this world rejoices Beholding the soul confounded; He delights to watch the death-throe of the heart. The gasping heart, at point of death, Seeks vain things, vainly searching; The flames clinging to the soul torture. The most disconsolate heart. The Rector of glooms rejoices To sacrifice the bitter heart; The King delights to sate the avid sisters And indulge their fury. *Alas! the Kingdom of Hell, Saith the King, shall not endure forever: But until the Heavenly kingdom come, I will give you victims.*

Dedicated to the philosopher and poet, George Santayana. In his autobiographical account, *The Middle Span* (1947), Santayana leaves us with a haunting description of Lionel's habitual tendency to live in dreams.

Dedication to Samuel Smith

Better than book of mine could be
Is this, where all enchantments blend,
This book of Celtic phantasy,
Made by the faeries and my friend.

A poet here will joy to find
The sorrow of the ancient seas;
The wailing of the wistful wind,
And all fair, strange things like to these.

The fire and dew of Irish dreams
Shine here within a twilight pale:
And in the magic twilight gleams
The secret soul of Inisfail.

1895

Inscription in a copy of W.B. Yeats' *The Celtic Twilight*
Lionel Johnson/London: 1893.
Sancte Ioannes de Cruce, Ora pro amico meo scriptori: ut in corpus
Christi Mysticum, ne pereat, intreat.

Our Lady of The May
To the Very Rev. Fr. Vassall, C.S.S.R

O Flower of flowers, our Lady of the May!
    Thou gavest us the World's one Light of Light:
Under the stars, amid the snows, He lay;
      While Angels, through the Galilean night
          Sang glory and sang peace:
          Nor does their singing cease,
For thou their Queen and he their King sit crowned
Above the stars, above the bitter snows;
They chaunt to thee the Lily, Him the Rose,
          With Saints kneeling round.
Gone is cold night: thine now are spring and day:
O Flower of flowers, our Lady of the May!

O Flower of flowers, our Lady of the May!
      Thou gavest us the blessed Christmas mirth:
And now, not snows, but blossoms, light thy way;
      We give thee the fresh flower-time of the earth.
         These early flowers we bring,
         Are angels of the spring,
Spirits of gracious rain and light and dew.
Nothing so like to thee the whole earth yields,
As these pure children of her vales and fields,
         Bright beneath skies of blue
Hail, Holy Queen! their fragrant breathings say:
O flower of flowers, our Lady of the May!

O Flower of flowers, our Lady of the May!
    Breathe from God's garden of eternal flowers
Blessing, when we thy little children pray:
    Let thy soul's grace steal gently over ours.
        Send on us dew and rain
        That we may bloom again,
Now wither in the dry and parching dust.
Lift up our hearts, till with adoring eyes,
O Morning Star! We hail thee in the skies,
        Star of our hope and trust!
Sweet star, sweet Flower, there bid thy beauty stay:
O Flower of flowers, our Lady of the May!

O Flower of flowers, our Lady of the May!
    Thou leftist lilies rising from thy tomb:
They shone in stately and serene array,
    Immaculate amid death's house of gloom.
        Ah, let thy graces be
        Sown in our dark hearts! We
Would make our hearts gardens for thy dear care;
Watered from wells of Paradise and sweet
With balm winds flowing from the Mercy Seat,
        And full of heavenly air:
While music ever in thy praise should play,
Of Flower of flowers, our Lady of the May!

O Flower of flowers, our Lady of the May!
Not only for ourselves we plead, God's Flower!
Look on thy blinded children, who still stray,
Lost in this pleasant land, thy chosen Dower!
     Send us a perfect spring:
     Let faith arise and sing,
And England from her long, cold winter wake.
Mother of Mercy! turn upon her need
Thine eyes of mercy: be there spring indeed:
     So shall thine Angels make
A starrier music, than our hearts can say,
O Flower of flowers, our Lady of the May!

Published in *The Catholic Magazine*, May 1st, 1895.

To Morfydd Dead

Morfydd at midnight
Met the Nameless Ones:
Now she wanders on the winds,
White and lone.
I would give the light
Of eternal suns,
To be with her on the winds,
No more lone!

Oh, wild sea of air!
Oh, night's vast sweet noon!
We would wander through the night,
Star and star.
Nay! but she, most fair!
Sun to me and moon:
I the vassal of her flight,
Far and far.

Morfydd at midnight
Met the Nameless Ones:
Now she wanders on the winds,
White and lone.
Take from me the light,
God! Of all Thy suns:
Give me her, who on the winds
Wanders lone!

1896

In Memory of Hubert Crackanthorpe

Requiescat in Pace
  Misierere Jesu!

Ours is the darkness, thine the light:
And yet the haunting thought of thee,
O fair and cordial friend! makes bright
The darkness; and we surely see
Thyself, thy very form and face
Filled with a fresh perfecting grace.

1897

Allegedly a relative of William Wordsworth, 36 year old Crackanthorpe is believed to have committed suicide by jumping into the Seine, in November 1896, after his marriage fell apart. The circumstances of Crackanthorpe's death have remained murky and foul-play was also rumoured. Hubert's aristocratic family attempted to hush up the unhappy episode and Crackanthorpe's literary legacy all but vanished as a consequence. Upon the passing of yet another cherished associate, Lionel, wrote to Louise Imogen Guiney: "On Christmas morning I heard of the death of a very great and dear friend, poor Hubert Crackanthorpe, the young story-writer." Johnson's brief but touching verse wasn't published until 1950, when it appeared in *The Poetry Review*.

Prologue

The May fire once on every dreaming hill
All the fair land with burning bloom would fill:
All the fair land, at visionary night,
Gave loving glory to the Lord of Light.
Have we no leaping flames of Beltaine praise
To kindle in the joyous ancient ways;
No fire of song, of vision, of white dream,
Fit for the Master of the Heavenly Gleam;
For him who first made Ireland move in chime,
Musical from the misty dawn of time?

Ah, yes: for sacrifice this night we bring
The passion of a lost soul's triumphing:
All rich with faery airs that, wandering long
Uncaught, here gather into Irish song;
Sweet as the old remembering winds that wail
From hill to hill of gracious Inisfail;
Sad as the unforgetting winds that pass
Over her children in her holy grass
At home, and sleeping well upon her breast,
Where snowy Deidre and her sorrows rest.

Another tale we tell you: how a man,
Filled with high dreams, his race of longing ran
Haunted by fair and infinite desire;
Whose life was music, yet a wounding fire.
Stern is the story: welcome it no less,

Aching and lofty in its loveliness.
Come, then, and keep with us an Irish feast,
Wherein the Lord of Light and Song is priest;
Now, as this opening of the gentle May
Watch warring passions at their storm and play;
Wrought with the flaming ecstasy of art,
Sprung from the dreaming of an Irish heart.

_____

First appeared in *Beltaine*, 1899, an Irish arts and theatre journal
edited by W.B. Yeats.

Ash Wednesday
In Memorium: Ernest Dowson

Memento, homo, quia, pulvis es!
To-day the Cross of Ashes marks my brow:
Yesterday, laid to solemn sleep wert thou,
O dear to me of old, and dearer now!
Memento, homo, quia pulvis es!

Memento, homo, quia pulvis es!
And all the subtile beauty of that face,
With all its winning, all its wistful grave,
Fades in the consecrated stilly place:
Memento, homo quia pulvis es!

Memento, homo, quia pulvis es!
The visible vehement earth remains to me;
The visionary quiet land holds thee:
But what shall separate such friends as we?
Memento, homo, quia pulvis es!

1900

One And All
In Memory of Alfred Ferrand

Thousands might die, and still to me it seem
   But a dim troubled dream,
Wherein the hastened beating of my heart
   Bare no profound pained part:
A visionary sorrow flying past!
    It bides with me, at last.
For now that fierce death hath taken him,
   Now those brave eyes are dim
Evermore; now that evermore hath he
   Left all he loved, and me;
Now that within the far-off earth he sleeps,
   While wife, while mother weeps:
My sorrow holds all sorrows by the hand,
   At verge of death's gray land;
Into my heart the thousand dead I take
   For his dear stricken sake;
They share with him, all his companion dead,
   The tears I cannot shed,
The love that goes in silence: they and he
   Seem as one friend, to me.

Published in *The Outlook*, January 20th, 1900.

Sancta Silverum
To the Earl Russell

Through the fresh woods there fleet
Fawns, with bright eyes, light feet:
Bright eyes, and feet that spurn
      The pure green fern.

Headed by leaping does,
The swift procession goes
Through thickets, over lawns:
      Followed by fawns.

Over slopes, over glades,
Down dells and leafy shades,
Away the quick deer troop:
      A wildwood group.

Under the forest airs,
A life of grace is theirs:
Courtly their look: they seem
      Things of a dream.

Some say, but who can say?
That a charmed troop are they:
Once youths and maidens white!
      These may be right.

(continued from previous page)

In 1904, W.B. Yeats selected and edited 21 of Lionel Johnson's poems for publication by the Dun Emer Press, Dundrum, Dublin. The original of 'Sancta Silverum' is considerably longer but loses momentum, hence Yeats' decision to edit the poem down to its finest and most delicate verses.

Francis 2nd Earl Russell edited *Some Winchester Letters* (1919) and was the Parliamentary under Secretary for India.

EPHEMERA

To
Dr. Sigerson
from
Lionel Johnson:
with respect and regard.

Inscription by Lionel Johnson to George Sigeron, in *The Second Book of the Rhymers' Club* (London: Elkin Mathews, 1892). Courtesy Mark Samuels Lasner Collection, University of Delaware Library.

Epitaphs in Cloisters

Epita. Georgii Flower in Artibus Magistri
Here sleeps George Flower: O fair and early flower!
      But oh! the sooner was that flower to fade.
Poor fourteen years a Fellow he: with power,
      Death's footstep called him hence, and he obeyed.

Tho. Welsted
Thomas Welsted lieth here,
Stricken at his eighteenth year.
Low death laid him, with a stone;
Now then, not to Oxford gone,
He hath entered Heaven instead.
First he was at School: now dead,
And to many mansions passed,
His place cannot be the last.

Extreme Unction
by Ernest Dowson, dedicated to Lionel Johnson.

Upon the eyes, the lips, the feet,
    On all the passages of sense,
The atoning oil is spread with sweet
    Renewal of lost innocence.

The feet that lately ran so fast
    To meet desire, are soothly sealed;
The eyes, that were so often cast
    On vanity, are touched and healed.

From troublous sights and sounds set free;
    In such a twilight hour of breath,
Shall once retrace his life, or see,
    Through shadows, the true face of death?

Vials of mercy! Sacring oils!
    I know not where nor when I come,
Nor through what wanderings and toils,
    To crave of you, Viaticum.

Yet, when the walls of flesh grow weak,
    In such an hour, it well may be,
Through mist and darkness, light will break,
    And each anointed sense will see.

1894

Extreme Unction is a last-rites ritual administered by a priest.

To Louise Imogen Guiney

7, Gray's Inn Square
Gray's Inn, London

March 30, 1898

My Dear Miss Guiney

First, a word of apology for my long silence, and acknowledgement of your kindliest letter in December. I have been grievously ill with repeated influenza, and attendant weaknesses of body and mind to a degree which has made all writing painful and almost impossible. I have not even had the energy to see the Hinksons, Meynells and others of our friends! It is nothing serious; but persistent mild malady tries me worse than dangerous illness: that can be bracing, this is worrying and wearying.

Now, to dear Aubrey Beardsley. Unhappily, I have not seen him since he became a Catholic: he has constantly been abroad, and he was no letter-writer, especially as his end drew near and inevitable. I fear then, that what I can say will hardly be of service. But I *can* say, emphatically, that his conversion was a spiritual work, and not an half insincere aesthetic act of change, not a sort of emotional experience or experiment: he became a Catholic with a true humility and exaltation of soul, prepared to sacrifice much. He withdrew himself from certain valued intimacies, which he felt incompatible with his faith: that implies much, in these days when artists so largely claim exemption, in the name of art, from laws and rules of life. His work, as himself declared, would have been very directly religious in scope and character: he would have dismissed from it all suggestion of anything dangerously morbid: he would have made it plain that he was sometimes a satirist of vices and follies and extravagancies, but not, so to say, a sentimental student of them for their curiosity and fascination's sake. There was always in him a vein of mental or imaginative unhealthiness and nervousness, probably due to his extreme physical fragility: this, he was setting himself to conquer, to transform into a spiritual and artistic source of energy. He died at twenty four: his whole work was done in some five or six years: he won extraordinary praise and blame: and only his personal friends can truly realise his inexpressibly frail hold upon life, during the few years of his passionate devotion to his art. His consciousness of imminent death – the certainty that whatever he might do in art, in thought, in life at all, must be done very soon, or never – forced him to face the ultimate questions. I do not for an instant mean that his conversion was a kind of feverish snatching at comfort and peace, a sort of anodyne or opiate for his restless mind: I only mean that, being under sentence of death, in the shadow of it, he was brought swiftly face to face with the values and purposes of life and of human activity, and that he "co-operated with grace", as theology puts it, by a more immediate and vivid vision of faith, than is granted to most converts. All that was best in his art, its often intense idealism, its longing to express the ultimate truths of beauty in line and form, its profound imaginativeness, helped to lead him straight to that faith which embraces and explains all human apprehensions of, and cravings for, the last and highest excellences. The eye of his body was quick to see: the eye of his soul was quickened to see. He was sorry, he said at the last, to die so young and leave his work unfinished: but he was "ready to obey God's Will". I believe that he had some thoughts of entering some order or congregation, in which he could have followed his art, and dedicated it directly to the service of the faith: in any case that was the temper or tendency of his thoughts towards the end. He was strangely gentle and winning, though passionate and vehement in his intellectual and aesthetic life: such passion and vehemence, tempered by his spiritual docility, might have achieved great and perfect things. As I have suggested, there was a side to his nature which might have led him far in the direction of technical excellence in the extreme, coupled with spiritual perversity in the extreme: he lived long enough to show that his course would have been otherwise. I ascribe all his work, which even great friends and admirers find unwelcome, partly to his febrile, consumptive, suffering state of body, with its consequent restlessness and excitability of mind: partly to sheer boyish insolence of genius, love of audaciousness, consciousness of power. He was often ridiculed, insulted, misconstrued: and he sometimes replied by extravagance. But despite all wantonness of youthful genius, and all the morbidity of disease, his truest self was on the spiritual side of things, and his conversion was true to that self. He was not the man to play with high things, still less with the highest of all: he would never have been a fantastical dilettante trifler with Catholicism, making it an emotional foil to other and base emotions. All the goodness and greatness in him, brought face to face with the last reality of death, leapt up to the sudden vision of faith, as their satisfaction and true end: and after a lingering period of strong daily pain, he died in quiet peace and happiness. Requiescat: with all my heart.

This, I think, is the strict truth: and if you can make the smallest use of it, I shall feel more than glad. But pray keep my name back: if you must give any sort of authority, merely say to Fr. Gasson, or others, that this comes from a Catholic friend of Beardsley and of yourself in England. If you think it worth copying out for Fr. Gasson, tell him that the writer has considered carefully every word: but that, if it conflict at all with other testimony, or contain anything which does not commend itself to him as a priest and director of souls, I do not profess to be absolutely in the right, but only to have given, with entire sincerity, my own strong impressions of the truth. Had I seen Aubrey since his reception, I might have sent you something of value: yet, since I knew him well, and talked much with him on many matters, and heard much of him, up to the last, from friends, I think my impression may at least give a suggestion that may be helpful. – Aubrey Beardsley, twenty-four: Hubert Crackenthorpe, twenty-six: my friends die young! …

I close abruptly, to catch the mail.

Ever sincerely yours,
Lionel Johnson.

Review of *The Countess Cathleen*

The Countess Cathleen is a play in four acts, and the date of its story is the later part of the sixteenth century: its heroine is the Countess, a lady who is lord over many followers and tenants. A famine is in the land: such a famine as that described by Spenser, a famine of so agonising an intensity that men and women go mad with suffering, lose their sense of natural and religious obligation, are ready to do and to dare all things to escape their torments. Two evil spirits, in the guise of rich merchants, come to buy the souls of the despairing people: the dread traffic goes briskly forward. The efforts of the Countess to stay the famine and save the people are frustrated by the demons: one hope remains. She will sell her pure soul – very precious in God's sight, and therefore in the devil's – in exchange for the souls of her people already bought, and for the money enough to buy them food. It is done: she makes, like Iphigenia, but in a loftier way, the sacrifice of herself. The souls of her people are redeemed from eternal death, their bodies relieved from the pangs of starvation. She dies, the saint self-doomed, with broken heart: angels descend from God to take her soul to Heaven, which is her reward for so supreme a loving sacrifice. The four acts are simple: the play moves with a plain impulse. There is no complexity, whether of facts or motives; it is in truth a narrative in dramatic form and a lyrical setting. We are not shown, but left to imagine, Cathleen's spiritual struggle: we are shown her passionate, pitying love for her people. They, in the irresponsible frenzy of suffering, are bartering their immortal souls for relief from temporal agony: she has an heroic love so strong that

Antient Concert Rooms

BRUNSWICK STREET, DUBLIN.

THE
IRISH LITERARY THEATRE

Under the auspices of the National Literary Society.

May 8th	. .	THE COUNTESS CATHLEEN: 8.30.
,, 9th	. .	THE HEATHER FIELD: 8.30.
,, 10th	. .	THE COUNTESS CATHLEEN: 3.0.
		THE HEATHER FIELD: 8.30.
,, 12th	. .	THE COUNTESS CATHLEEN: 8.30.
,, 13th	. .	THE HEATHER FIELD: 3.0.
		THE COUNTESS CATHLEEN: 8.30.

A Prologue by Mr. Lionel Johnson will be spoken at the First Performance.

General Manager	MISS FLORENCE FARR.
Treasurer	MR. EDWARD MARTYN.
Secretary	MRS. GEORGE COFFEY.
Stage Manager	MR. BEN WEBSTER.
Assistant Stage Manager	MR. BRENDON STEWERT.

Dresses and Wigs by NATHAN and CLARKSON.

Herr Bast's ' Suite on Irish Airs' (for String Quartet in 4 Movements) will be played before and between the acts each evening.
Violin and harp for incidental music.
Artistes : Mr. P. Delany, M. Ivors Cree, M. Grisard, Herr Bast, Miss Phyllis Paul (Harp).

she accepts, in the sight of God, the loss of her own soul, as a simple, sad act of self-sacrifice. The spiritual entanglement, the estimation of motives, the casuistry, unemphasised in the play itself, are present, as it were, in the minds of God, His saints and angels. It is the quite obvious, simple facts, that the play sets before us: how *this* was done, and *that*. Yet we never lose sight of the spiritual side of things: the dark, gross vapours of the rotting woods and marshes, poisonous and pestilent, are as the fumes and clouds of evil and sin: the purity and sincerity of Cathleen are as the spiritual brightness of faith and grace themselves. The play, with all its romantic strangeness, is finely and firmly upon the side of the higher life: the story of one who would lay down her life, not temporal but eternal, for her friends, by a divine excess of charity. It is full of imagination, humour, technical beauty; but the deepest impression upon the mind is this, that it tells a triumph of innocence, ready to endure all things, over the malicious cunning of evil.

In May 1899, Lionel's creative interpretation of W.B. Yeats' play *The Countess Cathleen* appeared in the inaugural edition of *Beltaine*, an "occasional" publication promoting Irish theatre and literature.

LIONEL JOHNSON - *INCURABLE*

Of Lionel Johnson: 1867–1902
By One Who Knew Him (Louise Imogen Guiney)

An early death has lately robbed the world of letters in England of its one critic of mark arisen in this generation. Poet-minds of the Arnold breed, with what may be called the hush of scholarship laid upon their full energies and animations, must necessarily grow rarer and rarer, in a society ever more noisy and more superficial. They cannot expect now the fostering cloistral conditions which were fully disturbed by the great Revolution. Yet they still find themselves here, in a state of royal dispossession, and live on as they can. Of these was Lionel Johnson. In criticism, though he seemed to care so little about acknowledging, preserving and collecting what he wrote, he was nobly able to "beat his music out"; his potential success lay there, perhaps, rather than in the exercise of his singularly lovely and austere poetic gift. But this is not saying he was more critic than poet. On the contrary, he was all poet; and the application of the poet's touchstone to human affairs, whether in art or in ethics, was the very thing which gave its extraordinary elasticity and balance to his prose work. Being what he was, a selfless intelligence, right judgement came easy to him and to set them down, at the eligible moment, was mere play. He had lived more or less alone from his boyhood, but alone with eternal thoughts and classic books. Whenever he spoke there was authority in the speech coloured by companionship with the great of his own election: with Plato; Lucretius and Virgil; Augustine; Shakespeare. His capacity for admiration was immense, though in the choice of what was admirable he was quite uncompromising. Beyond that beautiful inward

Ephemera

exaction "the chastity of honour," he was naturally inclined to
the charities of interpretation. He gave them, but he asked them
not, and would not thank you for your casual approval, except
by his all-understanding smile. Neither vanity, ambition, nor
envy ever so much as breathed upon him, and scholar that he
was, he had none of the limitations common to scholars, for he
was without fear, and without prejudice.

A striking feature in the make-up of his mind was its
interplay and counter-poise of contrasts. Full of worship and
wonder (and a certain devout sense of indebtedness kept him,
as by a strict rubric of his own, an allusive and a quoting writer)
he was also full of an almost fierce uninfluenced independence.
With a great vocabulary, his game was always to pack close, and
thin out, his words. Impersonal as Pan's pipe to the audience of
The Chronicle or *The Academy*, he became intensely subjective the
moment he reached his intimate sparsely inhabited fatherland
of poetry. His utterance, as daring in its opposite way as Mr.
John Davidson's, had laid bare some of the deepest secrets of
the spirit. And side by side with them, lie etched on the page
the most delicate little landscapes, each as happily conceived as
if "the inner eye" and "the eye on the object" of both of which
Wordsworth speaks, were one and the same.

One might have thought, misled by Lionel Johnson's
strongly philosophic fibre, his habits of a recluse simplicity,
his faith in minorities, his patrician old-fashioned tastes, that
he would have ranged himself with the abstract critics, with
Joubert and Vauvenargues, rather than with Sainte-Beuve.
But it was another of his surprising excellencies that he was
never out of tune with cosmic externals, and the aspirations
of today. Into these his brain had a sort of detached angelic

insight. His earliest book, published while he was very young, was not about some subtlety of Attic thought: it was a masterly exposition of *The Art of Thomas Hardy*. To have dwelt first with all divine exclusions for housemates, is to be safeguarded when Time drives one forth among its necessary acceptances and accretions. This same relevance and relativity of our friend, this open dealing with the nearest interest, was his strength; he not only did not shrink from contemporary life, but bathed in the apprehension of it as joyously as in a mountain-stream. How significant, how full of fresh force, have been his many unsigned reviews! Nothing so broad, so sure, so penetrating, has been said, in little, elsewhere, of such very modern men as Renan and William Morris.

It is perhaps less than exact to claim that Lionel Johnson had no prejudices. All his humilities and tolerances did not hinder his humorous depreciation of the Teutonic intellect; and he liked well King Charles II's word for it – "foggy." None-scientific, anti-mathematical, he was a genuine Oxonian: a recruit, as it were for transcendentalism and the White Rose. His studies were wilful and concentrated; he never tried to extend his province into a thorough understanding, for instance, of arts which he relished, like music and sculpture. And, discursive as his national sympathies certainly were, he was never out of the British Isles. In all such lateral matters, he saw the uses of repression, if his calling was to be not a dilettante impulse but the sustained and unwasted passion of a lifetime. Culture in him, it is truly needless to say, was not miscellaneous information; as in Newman's perfect definition, it was "the command over his own faculties, and the instinctive just estimate of things as they pass." He had an amazing and most accurate memory for everything worthwhile; it was as if he had moved, to some profit, in several ages, and forgotten none of their "wild and noble sights." And the powers which were so delighting to others, were in a reflex way, a most single-hearted and modest way, sheer delight to himself, chiefly because he had tamed them to his hand.

His non-professional conception of the function of a man of letters (only it was one of the thousand subjects on which he was sparing of speech, perhaps discouraged by insincerities of speech elsewhere) amounted to this: that he was glad to be a bondslave to his own discipline; that there should be no limit to the constraints and the labour self-imposed; that in pursuit of the best he would never count cost, never lower a pennon, never bow the knee to Baal. It was not his isolated position, nor his exemption from the corroding breath of poverty, which made it easy for such a one to hold his ground; for nothing can make easy that strenuous and entire consecration of a soul to what it is given to do. It extended to the utmost detail of composition. The proud melancholy charm of his finest stanzas rests upon the severest adherence to the laws and by-laws of rhythm; in no page of his was there ever a rhetorical trick or an underbred rhyme. Excess and show were foreign to him. The real shortcoming of his verse lies in its Latin strictness and asceticism, somewhat repellent to any readers but those of his own temper; or else in occasional paradoxical homeliness. Its emotional glow is a shade too moral, and it is only after a league of stately pacing that fancy is let go with a looser rein. Greater impeded in freedom of expression is that unblest poet who has historic knowledge of his own craft. To him, nothing is sayable which has already been well said. Lionel Johnson even as a beginner, was of so jealous an integrity that his youthful numbers, in their detail, are almost scandalously free from *parentalia*. It is not, surely, by some supernatural little joke that his most famous line,

Lonely unto the Lone, I go.

Had been anticipated by Plotinus? Here was a poet who liked the campaign better than Capua. He sought out voluntarily never, indeed, the fantastic, but the difficult way. If he could but work out his idea in music (easy as composition was to him) he preferred to do so with divers painstakings which less scrupulous vassals of the Muse would as soon practise fasting and praying. To one who looks well into the structure of his poems, they are like the roof of Milan Cathedral, "gone to seed with pinnacles", full of vowelled surprises and exquisitely devotional elaborations, given in the zest of service, and meant to be hidden from mundane eyes. Yet they have the grace to appear much simpler than they are. The groundwork, at least, is always simple; his usual metre is iambic or trochaic, and the English alexandrine he made his own. Precision clung like drapery to everything he did. His handwriting was unique: a slender, close slant, very odd, but most legible; a true script of the old time, without a flaw. It seemed to whisper: "Behold in me the inveterate foe of haste and discourtesy, of type-writers, telegrams and secretaries!" As he wrote, he punctuated: nothing was trivial to this "enamoured architect" of perfection. He cultivated a half-mischievous attachment to certain antique forms of spelling, and to the colon, which our slovenly press will have none of; and because the colon stood, and stands, for fine differentiations, and sly sequences, he delighted to employ it to tyrannize over printers.

Lionel Johnson's gallant thoroughness was applied not only to the department of literature. He had a loving heart, and laid upon himself the burden of many gratitudes. To Winchester, his old school, and Oxford, his university (in both of which he covered himself, as it happened, with honours) he was a bounden knight. The Catholic Church, to which he felt an attraction from infancy, and which he entered soon after he came of age, could command his whole zeal and furtherance, to the end. His faith was his treasure, and an abiding peace and compensation. The delicacy, nay, the sanctity of his character, was the outcome of it; and it so pervaded, guided and adjusted his whole attitude towards life (as Catholicism alone claims and intends to do) that his religiousness can hardly be spoken of, or examined as a thing separate from himself. There was a seal upon him as of something priestly and monastic. His place, like favourite Hawthornes, should have been in a Benedictine *scriptorium*, far away and long ago.

> Us the sad world rings round
>   With passionate flames impure:
> We tread an impious ground;
>   We hunger, and endure.

So he sang in one of his best known numbers. Meanwhile, the saints, bright from their earthly battle, and especially the angels, and Heaven their commonweal were always present to the imagination of this *anima naturaliter Christiana*. Again, his most conscious loyalty, with the glamour of medieval chivalry upon it, was for Ireland. He was descended from a line of soldiers, and from a stern soldier who, in the ruthless fashion of the time, put down at New Ross the tragic insurrection of 1798. Study and sympathy brought his great-grandson to see things from a point of view not in the least ancestral; and the consequence was that Lionel Johnson came to write, and even lecture, as the heart-whole champion of hapless Innisfail. In the acknowledged spirit of reparation, he gave his thoughts, his time, and his purse to her interests. He devoted his lyre to her, as his most moving theme, and he pondered not so much her political hope, nor the incomparable charm of her streams and valleys, as her constancy under sorrows, and the holiness of her mystical ideal. His inheritance was goodly unto him, for he had by race both the Gaelic and the Cymric strain, and his temperament, with its remoteness and its sage and sweet ironies, was by so much more and less than English. But he possessed also, in very full measure, what we nowadays perceive to be the basic English traits: deliberation, patience, and control. It was owing to these unexpected and saving qualities in him that he turned out no mere visionary, but made his mark in life like a man, and that he held out, for five-and-thirty years, in that fragile, terribly nervous body always so inadequate and perilous a mate for his giant intelligence.

Next to the impersonal allegiances which had so much claim upon him, was his feeling for his friends. The boy Lionel had been the exceptional sort of boy who can discern a possible halo about a master or a tutor; and at Oxford as at Winchester, he found men worth his homage. The very last poem he sent forth, only the other day, was a threnody for his dear and honoured Walter Pater, honoured and dear long after death, as during life. Like so much else from the same pen, it is of synthetic and illuminating beauty, and it ends with the tenderest of lyrical cries:

> Gracious God keep him; and God grant to me
>   By miracle to see
> That unforgettable most gracious friend,
>   In the never-ending end!

Friendship, with Lionel Johnson, was the grave, high, romantic sentiment of antique tradition. He liked to link familiar names with his own by means of little dedications, and the two volumes of his poems, with their placid blue covers and dignity of margin, furnish a fairly full roll-call of those with whom he felt himself allied: English, Irish, Welsh and American; men and women; famous and unknown; Christian and pagan; clerical and lay. It was characteristic of him that he addressed no poems directly to a friend, except once or twice, when well sheltered by a paraphrase, but set apart this or that, in print as private to one or another whose heart, he knew, would go along with it. As a proof of the shyness and reticence of his affections, it may be added that some who were fond of him did not discover for years after (and perhaps some have not yet discovered) the page starred with their own names, once given to them in silence, and for remembrance, by the hand which of late answered few letters, and withdrew more and more from social contact.

Alas, this brings us upon sad ground. We all first began to be conscious that something was wrong, and that we were losing him, nearly four years ago, when he shut himself up, and kept obstinate silence, for weeks and months, in the cloistral London nooks where he and his library successively abode.

Then, not quite two years ago, he had a painful and prolonged illness, in the course of which his hands and feet became wholly crippled; and for the ardent lover, in any weather, of the open countryside, arrived a dark twelvemonth of indoor inaction. It is to be feared that he was not properly nursed; he had never known how to care for himself, and had lived as heedless of the flesh as if he were all wings. It seemed ungenerous, that instinct to go into the dark at times, quite away from wanted intercourse. Yet it was neither ungenerous or perverse. Surging up the more as his bodily resources failed him, his old "mortal moral strife" had to be undergone: the fight in which there can be no comrades. The brave will in him fought long and fought hard: no victor could do more. He had apparently recovered his health after all the solitude and mental weariness, and had just expressed himself as "greedy for work," when he went out from his chambers in Clifford's Inn, late on the night of the 29th of September, for the last of his many enchanted walks alone: for with Hazlitt, against Stevenson, this walker held that any walk is the richer for being companionless. No one saw him faint or stumble and fall; but a policeman on his beat found the unconscious body against the curb in Fleet Street and had it carried to St. Bartholomew's Hospital. And there in the ward he lay, with his skull fractured (a child's skull it was abnormally thin, as the inquest showed) recognised and tended but always asleep, for four days and five nights; and then the little flickering candle went quietly out. In the bitter pathos of his end he was not with Keats, but with Poe. It was the 4th of October, 1902, a Saturday of misted autumn sunshine, sacred in the ecclesiastical calendar to the *Poverello* of Assisi. Of that blessed forerunner his dead poet had once written:

Thy loved all things, thy love knew no stay,
 But drew the very wild beasts round thy knee
O lover of the least and lowest! Pray,
 Saint Francis, to the Son of Man, for me.

The only other Englishman of letters so elfin-small and light
was De Quincey. Few persons could readily be got to believe
Lionel Johnson's actual age. With his smooth hair and cheek,
he passed for a slim undergrown boy of sixteen: his light-footed
marches, in bygone summers, over the Welsh hills and the
coasts of Dorset and Cornwall, were interrupted at every inn
by the ubiquitous motherly landlady, expostulating with him
for his supposed truancy. His extreme sense of humour forbade
annoyance over the episode; rather was it not unwelcome to one
who had no hold on time, and was as elemental as foam or air.
Yes, he lived and died young. It was not only simple country
folk who missed in him the adult "note." And yet a certain
quaint and courageous pensiveness of aspect and outlook; a hint
of power in the fine brow, the sensitive hands, the grey eye so
quick, and yet so chastened and incurious, could neither escape
a true palaeographer, nor be misconstrued by him. Lionel
Johnson must have been at all times both a man and a child. At
ten years old, or at the impossible sixty, he must equally have
gone on, in a sort of beautiful vital stubbornness, being a unit,
being himself. His manners, as well as his mental habits, lasted
him throughout; from the first he was a sweet gentleman and a
sound thinker. His earliest and latest poems, in kind altogether,
and largely in degree, were of a piece. A paper produced at
Winchester School, on Shakespeare's Fools, is as unmistakably
his as his final review of Tennyson. To put it rather roughly, he

had no discarded gods, and therefore no periods of growth. He was a crystal, a day-lily, shown without tedious processes. In his own phrase,

> All that he came to give
> He gave, and went again.

He had a homeless genius: it lacked affinity with the planetary influences under which he found himself here, being as Sir Thomas Browne grandly says, "older than the elements, and owing no homage unto the sun." He seemed ever the same because he was so. Only intense natures have this continuity with look and mood.

With all his deference, his dominant compassion, his grasp of the spiritual and the unseen, his feet stood foursquare upon rock. He was a tower of wholesomeness in the decadence which his short life spanned. He was no pedant, and no prig. Hesitations are gracious when they are unaffected, but thanks are due for the one among gentler critics of our passing hour who cared little to "publish his wistfulness abroad," and was clear as to what he would adore and what he would burn. He suffered indeed, but he won manifold golden comfort from the mercies of God, from human excellence, the arts, and the stretches of meadow, sky and sea. Sky and sea! they were sacrament and symbol, meat and drink, to him. To illustrate both his truth of perception when dealing with the magic of the natural world, and his rapturous sense of union with it, I am going to throw together, by a wholly irregular procedure, consecutive sections of three early and unrelated poems: one written at Cadgwith in 1892, one at Oxford in 1889, and the last (with its lovely opening anticipating of Tennyson) dating from Falmouth Harbour, as long ago as 1887.

1

Winds rush, and waters roll;
Their strength, their beauty brings
Into mine heart the whole
Magnificence of things:

That men are counted worth
A part upon this sea,
A part upon this earth,
Exalts and heartens me!

11

Going down the forest side
The night robs me of all pride,
By gloom and by splendour,
High, away, alone and afar,
Mighty wills and working are:
To them I surrender.

The processions of the night
Sweeping clouds and battling light,
And wild winds in thunder,
Care not for the world of man,
Passionate on another plan.
(O twin worlds of wonder!)

Ancients of dark majesty
Priests of splendid mystery
The Powers of Night cluster:
In the shadows of the trees,
Dreams that no man lives and sees,
The dreams! The dreams! muster.

111

I have passed over the rough sea,
And over the white harbour bar,
And this is death's dreamland to me,
Led hither by a star.

And what shall dawn be? Hush thee: nay!
Soft, soft is night, and calm and still.
Save that day cometh, what of day
Knowest thou, good or ill?

Content thee. Not the annulling light
Of any pitiless dawn is here:
Thou art alone with ancient night,
And all the stars are clear.

Only the night air and the dream;
Only the far sweet-smelling wave;
The stilly sounds, the circling gleam,
Are thine; and thine a grave.

Surely, no pity need be wasted upon one who resolved himself into so glorious a harmony with all creation, and with the mysteries of our mortal being. To be happy is a feat nothing less than heroic in our complex air. Snow-souled and fire-hearted, sentient and apprehensive, Lionel Johnson, after all and in spite of all, dared to be happy. As he never worried himself about awards, the question of his tomorrow's station and his measure of fame need not obtrude upon a mere mental character study. Memorable and exhilarating has been the ten-years' spectacle of him in unexhausted free play, now with his harp, now with blunted rapier, under the steady dominion of a genius so wise and so ripe that one knows not where in living companies to look for its parallel. Well: may we soon get used to thinking of our dearest guild-fellow in a safer City, where no terror of defeat can touch him!

"And he shall sing There according to the days of his youth, and according to the days of his going up out of the land of Egypt."

L.I.G.

Lionel Johnson's notes in his copy of Christina Rossetti's *New Poems: Hitherto Unpublished or Uncollected*, edited by William Michael Rossetti (London; New York: Macmillan and Co. 1896). Courtesy Mark Samuels Lasner Collection, University of Delaware Library.

IN MEMORIAM LIONELLI JOHNSON UTRIUSQUE COLLEGII
B. MARIÆ WINTON. OLIM SCHOLARIS. HUIUS LOCI DUM VIXIT
AMANTISSIMI. QUI BONARUM OMNIUM LITTERARUM PERITUS
ÆSTIMATOR INTER POETAS IPSE WICCAMICOS HAUD MINIMUS
HABEBITUR. NATUS EST DIE XV. MARTII ANNO SAL. MDCCCLXVII
OBIIT LONDINII DIE IV. OCT. MDCCCCII. REQUIESCAT IN PACE.

Above: a brass tablet honouring Lionel Johnson was unveiled in the cloisters of Winchester College in 1904, following a campaign by the poet's friends, both literary and Wykehamical, to enshrine his memory.

Dedications:

Through long twilights linden scented:
Caspar Wintermans & Louise Imogen Guiney (1861-1920).

Wanderings by old-world ways:
Timothy D'Arch Smith, Mark Samuels Lasner, Suzanne Foster, Julia Marlow Thomas, Godfrey Brangham & Mark Valentine.

STRANGE ATTRACTOR PRESS 2024

Printed in the United States
by Baker & Taylor Publisher Services